THE POLES IN BRITAIN 19

Also by Peter D. Stachura

Nazi Youth in the Weimar Republic (Santa Barbara and Oxford: ABC Clio, 1975)
The Weimar Era and Hitler: A Critical Bibliography (Oxford: ABC Clio, 1977)
The Shaping of the Nazi State (editor) (London: Croom Helm, 1978)
The German Youth Movement, 1900–1945: An Interpretative and Documentary History
    (London: Macmillan, 1981)
The Nazi Machtergreifung (editor) (London: Allen & Unwin, 1983)
Gregor Strasser and the Rise of Nazism (London: Allen & Unwin, 1983)
Unemployment and the Great Depression in Weimar Germany (editor) (London:
    Macmillan, 1986)
The Weimar Republic and the Younger Proletariat: An Economic and Social Analysis
    (London: Macmillan, 1989)
Themes of Modern Polish History (editor) (Glasgow: Polish Social and Educational
    Society, 1992)
Political Leaders in Weimar Germany: A Biographical Study (New York: Simon &
    Schuster, 1993)
Poland Between the Wars, 1918–1939 (editor) (London: Macmillan, 1998)
Poland in the Twentieth Century (London: Macmillan, 1999)
Perspectives on Polish History (editor) (Stirling: Centre for Research in Polish
    History, 2001)

THE POLES IN BRITAIN
1940–2000
From Betrayal to Assimilation

Editor

PETER D. STACHURA

University of Stirling

Foreword by Dr Stanisław Komorowski
Ambassador of the Republic of Poland to Great Britain

FRANK CASS
LONDON • PORTLAND, OR

First Published in 2004 in Great Britain by
FRANK CASS PUBLISHERS
Crown House, 47 Chase Side
London N14 5BP

and in the United States of America by
FRANK CASS PUBLISHERS
c/o ISBS, 920 NE 58th Avenue, Suite 300
Portland, Oregon, 97213-3786

Website http://www.frankcass.com

Copyright chapters © 2004 contributors
Copyright collection © 2004 Frank Cass & Co. Ltd

British Library Cataloging in Publication Data:

The Poles in Britain, 1940–2000: from betrayal to assimilation
1. Poles – Great Britain – History – 20th century – Congresses
2. World War, 1939–1945 – Participation, Polish – Congresses
I. Stachura, Peter D.
305.8'9185041'09045

ISBN 0-7146-5562-7 (cloth)
ISBN 0-7146-8444-9 (paper)

Library of Congress Cataloging-in-Publication Data:

Stachura, Peter D.
    The Poles in Britain, 1940–2000: from betrayal to assimilation/
    editor, Peter D. Stachura.
        p. cm
    Includes bibliographical references and index.
    ISBN 0-7146-5562-7 – ISBN 0-7146-8444-9 (pbk)
        1. Poles–Great Britain–History–20th century. 2. Immigrants–
        Great Britain–History–20th century. 3. Great Britain–Ethnic
        relations–History–20th century.
    I. Title.
    DA125.P6S79 2003
    941'.0049185–dc22

                                                            2003055417

Typeset in 11/13 pt New Baskerville
by Cambridge Photosetting Services, Cambridge
Printed in Great Britain by MPG Books Ltd, Victoria Square, Bodmin, Cornwall

For Kay, Gregory and Madeleine

Contents

Foreword

The group of scholars under Professor Peter Stachura's supervision
has succeeded in writing an extremely interesting book which fills a
gap in the English-language historiography. It also throws new light
on hitherto unknown facts of Polish history. The objective attitude
of the authors towards the Polish community in Britain needs to be
praised even more, if one keeps in mind the subjective analysis made
by others of some events in Polish history.

The authors' initiative should also be appreciated because for
many decades the Polish soldiers of 1939 have not been granted
adequate recognition, not only from the former Polish communist
government – which is clearly demonstrated in the book – but also
from the British side. Their heroic struggle 'For Your and Our
Liberty', in accordance with a long-established Polish tradition,
began with the German and Russian aggression of September 1939.
It finished on the territory of the United Kingdom.

Nevertheless, as the authors show, the end of the Second World
War cannot be considered as the closure of the battle for an independent Poland. The reality of the post-Yalta world order forced
many of the ex-soldiers to become immigrants. During the entire
communist period in Poland, they continued to cultivate in exile
Polish culture, with its values and spirit. They maintained markedly
high standards of patriotism and devotion. In spite of initial difficulties, internecine animosities and, often, antipathy from some British
circles, they never gave up hope of returning to a free country. Some
of them have now managed to visit newly independent Poland, and
continue to contribute, through their own activities, to improving its
image in Britain.

Having mentioned the Polish soldiers, one ought not to forget
their descendants born and raised in the United Kingdom. Many of
them are proud of their heritage, and their favourable attitude
towards Poland needs to be fully acknowledged.

I would like to express my gratitude to the authors of the book.
Thanks to them, the work of the Polish community in the United

Kingdom, and particularly of the wartime immigrants, has been recognised and highly rated.

I am persuaded that by introducing an English-speaking readership to a subject as interesting as the last sixty years in the life of the Polish community – one of the most numerous ethnic groups in the United Kingdom – the authors significantly promote an improvement in common understanding, tolerance and openness among members of British society.

Dr Stanisław Komorowski
Ambassador of the Republic of Poland to Great Britain
June 2003

Acknowledgements

All but one of the contributions in this book originated as papers at the conference 'The Poles in Britain, 1940–2000: New Research', which was organised on 2 March 2001 by the Centre for Research in Polish History, University of Stirling. A large and appreciative audience stimulated some vigorous debate, which I found most gratifying.

I should like to thank the M. B. Grabowski Fund and the Polonia Aid Foundation Trust, both of London, for their generous sponsorship of the Centre, including its conferences, since its inception on 3 May 2000. Additional funding for this most recent conference was kindly provided by the Royal Historical Society and the Faculty of Arts, University of Stirling.

Of the many individuals who have taken a sustained interest in my work with the Centre, I should like to mention, in particular, Professor Sir Ian Kershaw, University of Sheffield, and Dr Bob McKean, Head of the Department of History, University of Stirling.

Peter D. Stachura
Bridge of Allan
Polish Independence Day, 2002

Notes on Contributors

Jeffrey Bines is a Ph.D. student at the Centre for Research in Polish History, University of Stirling, researching the Polish Section of the Special Operations Executive in the Second World War. He is the author of *Operation Freston. The British Military Mission to Poland, 1944* (1999).

Kathy Burrell is a Lecturer in History at De Montfort University. Her doctoral research focuses on the Polish, Italian and Greek-Cypriot communities in post-war Leicester.

Evan McGilvray, a graduate of the School of Slavonic and East European Studies, University of London, completed a Master's degree at the University of Bradford in 2000 and is currently a Ph.D. student at the University of Leeds. His book, *The Black Devils*, a history of the First Polish Armoured Division in the Second World War, is forthcoming.

Wojciech Rojek is Director of the Historical Institute at the Jagiellonian University, Kraków, and the author/editor of several publications relating to the Polish government-in-exile in London after 1945.

Peter D. Stachura is Professor of Modern European History and Director of the Centre for Research in Polish History, University of Stirling. He is a specialist in Modern German and Polish history, and his most recent major publications are *Political Leaders in Weimar Germany. A Biographical Study* (1993), *Poland Between the Wars, 1918–1939* (editor), (1998), *Poland in the Twentieth Century* (1999) and *Perspectives on Polish History* (editor), (2001). He is a Fellow of the Royal Historical Society.

Andrzej Suchcitz is Keeper of Archives at the Polish Institute and Sikorski Museum, London. His primary research interest is in modern

Polish military history, on which he has written, edited and co-edited a number of books and articles. He is a member of several editorial committees, including that of *Teki Historyczne*, published by the Polish Historical Society in Great Britain, and is a Fellow of the Royal Historical Society.

Michelle Winslow completed her doctorate at the University of Sheffield in 2001, where she is now a Research Associate. She is co-author (with Tim Smith) of *Keeping the Faith. The Polish Community in Britain* (2000).

List of Plates

These photographs have been kindly provided by Mr Andrzej Suchcitz from the Archive of the Polish Institute and Sikorski Museum, London, and by Mrs Sarah Stachura and Professor Peter Stachura from their private collections.

Abbreviations

ACRPH	Archive of the Centre for Research in Polish History
AK	Home Army
APISM	Archive of the Polish Institute and Sikorski Museum
BBC	British Broadcasting Corporation
FDM	Federation of Democratic Movements
HCD	House of Commons Debates
GHQ	General Headquarters
JCC	Joint Consultative Committee
Lt.-Col.	Lieutenant-Colonel
MI	Military Intelligence
MP	Member of Parliament
NAS	National Archives of Scotland
NKVD	Soviet Secret Police
PAFT	Polonia Aid Foundation Trust
PCNU	Provisional Council of National Unity
PDA	Polish Democratic Alliance
PNDC	Polish National Democratic Committee
PPS	Polish Socialist Party
PRC	Polish Resettlement Corps
PRO	Public Record Office
PSL	Polish Peasants' Party
RAF	Royal Air Force
SIS	Secret Intelligence Service
SN	National Party (Polish)
SP	Labour Party (Polish)
SOE	Special Operations Executive
SPK	Polish Ex-Combatants' Association
TUC	Trades Union Congress
UB	Polish Secret Police (communist, post-1945)
UK	United Kingdom
USA	United States of America
VE	Victory in Europe

1

Introduction

Peter D. Stachura

The extreme volatility and tragedy of Poland's history since at least the Partitions of the eighteenth century have produced frequent episodes of enforced emigration and deportation for millions of Poles. Already by the middle of the nineteenth century, particularly in the wake of the unsuccessful risings of 1830 and 1863 against Russian oppression, large-scale displacement had become a salient characteristic of Polish life. At the very heart of this trauma lay the primary challenge of how to regain Poland's freedom and independence as a national sovereign state. This theme provides the essential line of continuity in Polish history in the modern era. In the second half of the nineteenth century, this challenge was addressed initially, and principally, through the process known as 'organic work', the promotion, as far as was possible within the restrictive regime imposed by the Partionist powers, of the Polish economy, language, religion, culture, education and social traditions. In the latter decades of the century, new avenues towards the same goal were pursued, notably through a revolutionary, anti-tsarist brand of socialism and a militant form of nationalism, epitomised by Józef Piłsudski and Roman Dmowski, respectively.

Nevertheless, by the eve of the First World War, some five million Poles had already made their way to the United States, compelled to emigrate by economic adversity and political discrimination. Much smaller Polish communities had also emerged in various European countries, including France, Germany and Belgium. The movement of Poles on such a scale ceased only during the inter-war phase of the Second Republic. This is to be explained by the profound sense of patriotic commitment felt by most Poles at having recovered their independence at last and, equally, by the fact that the Republic, in the face of the most daunting internal and external problems and impediments, proved capable of outstanding achievements in many important spheres. Poles had not experienced such a quality of life, pride and self-respect for well over a hundred years.

The successful course of the Second Republic was crudely shattered in September 1939 by the combined invasion and occupation of Poland by National Socialist Germany and the Communist Soviet Union, the two most nefarious regimes in twentieth-century Europe. Both Germany and the Soviet Union had, of course, been Poland's implacable adversaries since the Treaty of Versailles, in 1919. But it was under the totalitarian dictators, Adolf Hitler and Josef Stalin, that their hatred of Poland acquired an unprecedented level of intensity. Notwithstanding their positions at opposite ends of the political and ideological spectrum, the two countries were infamously drawn together in a pact to destroy their mutual enemy. They ignored, however, one very significant point, familiar to any serious student of Polish history. That is, regardless of the most inauspicious circumstances, the Poles always, without fail, find a way to continue the fight. National tradition dictates that this should be so.

Accordingly, in the aftermath of the heroic but doomed resistance of the Polish Armed Forces in the September campaign, thousands of troops managed to regroup abroad with the sole aim of continuing the struggle for Poland's freedom – in effect, to turn a temporary defeat into final victory, alongside their allies. In June 1940, immediately after the fall of France, Polish soldiers, air and naval personnel began arriving in Britain. Their history during and after the Second World War is the subject of this book.

The English-language historiography of this theme has been fairly limited hitherto, and consists, in the main, of articles in scholarly journals, chapters in anthologies, published lectures and memoirs. However, a small number of monographs has been written and has provided something of a platform for this latest collection of essays. In the first instance, the late Keith Sword's contributions deserve special mention. His *The Formation of the Polish Community in Great Britain, 1939–1950* (in collaboration with Norman Davies and Jan Ciechanowski), published by the School of Slavonic and East European Studies (SSEES) at the University of London in 1989, is a pioneering effort, packed with generally reliable factual information, even if limited in analysis and argument. Sword's 1996 sequel, *Identity in Crisis. The Polish Community in Britain*, also published by the SSEES, concentrates on the Polish experience in England in the

1990s, although it does situate this theme in a broader historical context. In addition, the sociologically oriented studies by Jerzy Zubrzycki, *Polish Immigrants in Britain. A Study of Adjustment* (The Hague, 1956), and *Soldiers and Peasants: The Sociology of Polish Migration* (SSEES, 1988), furnish valuable insights. Future works will endeavour to expand upon the lines of enquiry initiated by these contributions, not only by providing further detail but also by examining different aspects of the Polish émigré experience in this country.

The fundamental basis and unifying theme of the present work are the impact on Poles of the Second World War and the political settlement at its conclusion, above all the international conference at Yalta in February 1945. If the war caused large numbers of Poles to come to Britain, the decisions taken by the 'Big Three' allies – the United States, Britain and the Soviet Union – at Yalta caused most of them to remain here and to begin the task of establishing yet another Polish community on foreign soil. This outcome, and the reasons behind it, are made explicit in the first chapter, by Peter Stachura, who argues that soon after the Soviet Union joined the Western Allies in the fight against Hitler, the cause of a Free Poland was increasingly and inexorably lost. While the Polish government in London was not without its faults, the aims it represented as the legitimate and officially recognised successor to the government that collapsed in Poland in September 1939, came to be regarded as inconvenient and then expendable within the evolving context of international power politics. Consequently, in 1945, Poland was effectively abandoned by its erstwhile British and American allies to the Soviet Union and communism. All this was also despite the noteworthy military contribution that the Polish forces had made to ultimate Allied victory. Although most of the details of that contribution are already part of the historical record, Jeffrey Bines, in his chapter, throws light on an aspect that is not widely appreciated – the Polish role in the Special Operations Executive. He explains how this role was conceived and organised in the first years of the war.

The consequences of the war and its outcome for the Poles in Britain are examined in the remaining chapters in this book. Most are related to the question of how they adjusted and settled down in the post-war era in different parts of the country. In the first instance, the Polish government-in-exile in London would have been expected to emerge as a major point of orientation for the Poles. Unfortunately, that did not materialise. Wojciech Rojek reveals the deep divisions that quickly engulfed this derecognised (from July 1945) and largely isolated Polish government after 1945. The incessant personality clashes and organisational splits that occurred within it further undermined its status and efficacy, not merely within the Polish community that was taking shape, but also in the international arena, where it aspired to have a voice. Hence, the government's principal objective, to recreate Poland as a free and independent state once again, was eventually achieved far more as a result of the dramatic events in Poland itself during the 1980s, with particular reference to the rise of *Solidarność* (Solidarity).

Peter Stachura's second contribution, and those by Kathy Burrell and Michelle Winslow, illustrate the formidable difficulties the Poles faced as they sought to carve out a new life in this country. In Scotland, early wartime admiration for the Poles was replaced by a hostility extending at least into the early post-war years. Before the end of the war the Poles were experiencing political opposition, for different reasons, from the British government, the media, trade unions and Labour Party. The latter two organisations, where sympathy and even active support for the Soviet Union and communism was strong, were to the forefront of a campaign to denigrate the Poles as right-wing reactionaries and anti-Semites. Endemic anti-Catholic sectarianism compounded the issue in certain parts of Scotland, as did, nationally, post-war competition for jobs, housing and food. The terror-led consolidation of the Soviet-backed communist regime in Warsaw was a further source of unhappiness for the Poles, whose future in Scotland from the perspective of 1950 was hardly encouraging.

Burrell and Winslow have employed oral history techniques and methodologies in their separate consideration of the first generation of the Polish communities that were established in Leicester and elsewhere. With remarkable poignancy, they reveal the traumatic effect the war and its aftermath had on these now elderly Poles, many of whom suffered mental illness as a consequence. Both chapters pose important questions about the nature and extent of the Poles' assimilation.

The difficulties for the Poles discussed in these three chapters are illuminated by Evan McGilvray in regard to one very prominent figure in the post-war Polish community, that of General Stanisław Maczek, the Commander of the Polish First Armoured Division

1942–45. Despite his status as a highly decorated war hero and as the unofficial leader of the Polish community in Scotland, General Maczek was treated in the most appalling fashion by the British authorities after 1945. Prematurely retired from the Polish Army and denied appropriate civilian employment, he was forced to live a modest lifestyle that was the antithesis of his former professional and social status. Many other Poles of broadly similar background suffered the same fate, but none had enjoyed the prestige or authority of General Maczek, which makes his case all the more sad and disagreeable. Nevertheless, whatever difficulties he and his fellow Poles and their families had to confront, he continued to personify in a vibrant and wholly admirable manner the cause of a Free Poland.

Many of these chapters, besides making an informed statement on their own account, also indicate to one degree or another the potential for further research into the formation of the Polish community from 1940 onwards. Appropriately, therefore, the final contribution to this volume, by Andrzej Suchcitz, delineates the impressive array of materials that are available to researchers in the Archive of the Polish Institute and Sikorski Museum. It is particularly abundant in documentation relating to the Polish Armed Forces and to the wartime and post-war Polish government in London, including the war diary of General Władysław Sikorski, and papers, memoranda and correspondence from the Presidential Office, the Cabinet, important ministries and prominent individuals. Clearly, the Archive must now be regarded as not only the most important for modern Polish history in the United Kingdom, but also one of genuine international stature.

It is to be hoped overall that this work, in examining various interrelated aspects of a fresh and distinctive chapter in the history of the Polish *Emigracja*, provides the reader with an informative, coherent and objective survey of how the Polish community in Britain developed. If, at the same time, it stimulates and intimates the way towards further detailed research, so much the better. In essence, the Polish experience has displayed both positive and negative features, as the contributors reveal, which will doubtless provoke debate and different interpretations of where the balance should lie. What is beyond all dispute, however, is that at the core of this evolving experience lay the shameless treachery of Yalta.

2

Towards and Beyond Yalta

Peter D. Stachura

The Yalta Conference in February 1945 was the defining moment in the development of the Polish émigré community in Britain. Before the Second World War, the few Poles in this country hardly constituted a community and were invariably, in any case, Jewish refugees from earlier tsarist persecution who did not necessarily regard themselves as being Polish at all.[1] The Polish forces who began arriving here from 1940 fully expected to return home once the war was over and won. Yalta radically and irrevocably changed all that.

A principal concern of the Allied statesmen at the conference had been the post-war fate of Poland. The discussions involving President Franklin D. Roosevelt (1882–1945) of the United States, Prime Minister Winston Churchill (1874–1965) of Great Britain and Marshal Joseph Stalin (1879–1953) of the Soviet Union resulted, firstly, in the adoption, with minor adjustments, of the so-called 'Curzon Line' as Poland's new eastern border.[2] This meant that almost half of its pre-war territory, including the historically Polish cities of Wilno and Lwów, was to be incorporated into the Soviet Union, with Poland 'compensated', so to speak, with German territory in the north and west.[3] Poland was thus to be physically moved several hundred miles to the west, and to end up smaller in size and population (after allowing for war losses) and much different in geographical shape, compared with 1939.

The statesmen also agreed to the creation of a Provisional Government of National Unity in Warsaw 'on a broader democratic basis with the inclusion of democratic leaders from Poland itself and from Poles abroad', with 'free and unfettered elections as soon as possible on the basis of universal suffrage and secret ballot'.[4] Churchill assured the House of Commons that 'Stalin and the Soviet leaders wish to live in honourable friendship and equality with the Western democracies. I feel also that their word is their bond. I know of no Government which stands to its obligations ... more solidly than the Russian Soviet Government.'[5] Stalin himself stated at Yalta that 'it is not only a question of honour for Russia, but one of absolute necessity, to have Poland independent, strong and democratic'.[6]

The reaction to the Yalta decisions of the Polish government, which had been housed in London since the fall of France in June 1940 and had been a faithful ally against Nazi Germany throughout the war, was immediately and unreservedly denunciatory. It talked of 'betrayal' and of 'a sell-out' by its erstwhile allies. The Poles complained, understandably, that they had not even been invited to participate in the conference and had not at any stage been consulted about its deliberations, in 'contradiction of the elementary principles binding the Allies' and in 'violation of the letter and spirit of the Atlantic Charter and the right of every nation to defend its own interest'.[7]

Furthermore, the Polish government declared that the Yalta decisions on Poland 'cannot be recognised ... and cannot bind the Polish Nation', adding that 'the severance of the Eastern half of the territory of Poland' was 'a fifth partition ... now accomplished by the Allies'. The Poles also vehemently objected to the creation of the Provisional Government of National Unity because such a move 'can only legalise Soviet interference in Polish internal affairs'.[8] In any case, it was intimated, the Polish government in London had been recognised by the Western Allies since 1940 as the legitimate representative of the Polish nation.

More bitter recriminations followed, and not only from Polish leaders such as the Polish Foreign Minister, Adam Tarnowski, politicians and the outstanding military commander, General Władysław Anders (1892–1970).[9] Other observers of Polish affairs joined in the outpouring of anger. For example, Arthur Bliss Lane (1894–1956), the American Ambassador to Poland 1944–47, lamented the American and British 'capitulation' over Poland to the Soviets, criticising Roosevelt, in particular, for being 'no match for the wily, tough Stalin', and consequently for being 'outwitted, outmanoeuvred and outfoxed'.[10] Sir Owen O'Malley (1887–1974), British Ambassador to Poland 1941–45, wrote a scathing critique of Britain's treatment of the Poles.[11] These were all futile, however, and to add further insult to grievous injury, the Allies withdrew their recognition of the London-based Polish government in July 1945.[12]

A former Polish Army officer accurately captured the mood of his comrades on the ground, as it were, when he later recalled:

> After having endured so much pain, suffering and sacrifice … we were dumbfounded and bitterly resentful when news of the settlement reached us. Some just stared into the empty space unable to speak, others wept openly, while others still raised their voices in anger and recrimination. How could our British allies and friends betray us so shamefully? For us, Churchill now appeared to be an unscrupulous, deceitful rascal.[13]

It is beyond dispute that the Polish national interest, as defined and represented throughout the war by the Polish government in London, was shamelessly ignored at Yalta. In view of her huge territorial losses and the imposition of a Soviet-backed communist regime – in a country where before the war the Communist Party had, of course, only minimal popular support[14] – which soon established a reign of terror, Poland was indeed betrayed by her war-time allies. Paradoxically, then, while being on the so-called 'winning side' of the war, Poland ended up as one of the main losers. Indeed, it was treated as severely as defeated Germany, which had caused the war. On the face of it, such a perverse outcome seems inexplicable, until, that is, developments from 1941 onwards among both the Allies and the Polish government are taken into account. Accordingly, it must be asked how realistic Polish expectations were of Yalta.

When the Polish government and troops began arriving in Britain in 1940, they were feted as 'gallant allies' in the fight against Hitler (1889–1945) and accorded a great deal of sympathy, friendship and hospitality, particularly in Scotland, where the bulk of the Polish troops were soon encamped.[15] Churchill admired and cooperated well with their leader, General Władysław Sikorski (1881–1943), even if he soon formed a low opinion of most other members of his government, whom he thought difficult and irritating.[16] However, Britain and Poland had never been natural allies, and the very serious problems faced by the Poles in the years ahead possibly originated in the pre-war period. For instance, Britain had been a late convert to the idea of setting up an independent Polish state in 1918, and was later critical of what it saw as Polish expansionism in

Eastern Europe. Contrary to some views,[17] Britain's Prime Minister, David Lloyd George (1863–1945), was noticeably ill-disposed towards the Poles. He favoured the Germans in the acrimonious dispute over Upper Silesia in 1919–22, and, as a private citizen, actually welcomed the Soviet invasion of Poland in September 1939. Poland's main ally after 1918 had been France, and a Polish embassy was not established in London until 1929. In the 1930s, and particularly during the era of appeasement, Britain, whose chief concern was its Empire, regarded Eastern Europe as being composed of 'far-away' countries, as Prime Minister Neville Chamberlain (1869–1940) once remarked, notoriously, of Czechoslovakia. Moreover, Poland's image had been tarnished, in the eyes of many international observers, by what was perceived to be her political instability, poor relations with her ethnic minorities, especially the Jews, and delusions of 'great power' status.[18] The Anglo-Polish Treaty of August 1939 represented, therefore, a striking departure from the usual relations between both countries during the inter-war period.

In 1940, Britain and Poland were brought together only by unprecedented circumstances of adversity: the one had already been attacked and occupied by Nazi Germany, while the other was under direct threat of experiencing the same. Strangely, but ominously, the Soviet invasion and occupation of Poland, also in September 1939, was given relatively little publicity in Britain, in case, presumably, it would somehow detract from focusing on Germany as the common enemy. It may also have had something to do with the considerable reservoir of pro-Soviet and communist sympathy among significant sections of academia, the media and other agencies that shaped what was then rather euphemistically described as 'public opinion' in this country.

Despite the goodwill of those early days of the war, however, the balance of power in the Anglo-Polish relationship was firmly in favour of the host country, not least because the Poles were exiles with very limited contact with their homeland, had relatively few military resources and personnel, and were financially dependent on Britain. Also, leading British spokesmen made clear from the beginning that Britain would not guarantee Poland's eastern border with the Soviet Union – an attitude that subsequently had the most serious political and diplomatic implications for the Poles.[19]

The Poles' situation began to deteriorate decisively immediately after the German attack (Operation Barbarossa) on the Soviet Union, in summer 1941. With these two former allies in the occupation and destruction of Poland (1939–41) now the most implacable of enemies, Churchill resolved to bring Stalin into the anti-Nazi coalition and to make as many concessions as it took to keep him there. The formation of the Grand Alliance in 1942 at once relegated the Polish government to junior status, as the Soviet Union's interests and ambitions in Eastern Europe were to be accommodated repeatedly by Britain and the United States. Although Sikorski was himself apparently keen to reach an understanding with the Soviets after 1941, despite powerful opposition from important members of his own government, it was Churchill, who, in the interests of Allied unity, was the driving force behind the Soviet–Polish Pact in July 1941.[20] But, although the Pact re-established diplomatic relations between the two countries and allowed the formation of a Polish army from Polish prisoners in the Soviet Union, it did not, crucially, include Soviet acceptance of the pre-war border with Poland, as defined by the Treaty of Riga (1921), which had concluded the Polish-Soviet Bolshevik War.[21]

Sikorski, who was disliked and distrusted from the outset by many of his fellow-Polish exiles in Britain, notably the largely Piłsudskiite army officer corps, found it increasingly difficult to hold his government together,[22] particularly after the 1941 Pact, and as Stalin's position in the Grand Alliance was strengthened by his victories at Stalingrad and Kursk in 1943. The Soviet leader was then seen to be winning the war in the vital Eastern Front. This fact was brutally brought home to the Poles when, in April 1943, Stalin felt confident enough to sever diplomatic relations with Sikorski's government in the immediate aftermath of the discovery of the Katyń massacre of Polish officers, and to forge ahead with his longstanding plans to make good the Soviet losses at Riga and to install at the end of the war a communist regime in Poland loyal to the Soviet Union.[23] Shortly afterwards, in July, the Poles suffered yet another crushing blow when Sikorski, a leader of genuine stature, notwithstanding his much-diminished influence with the Allies, died in a still unsatisfactorily explained plane crash off Gibraltar. Even then, however, the political and diplomatic imperatives of the war effort had already bypassed the Poles. Any lingering doubts about this were completely dispelled by the decisions taken about Poland's future – in the absence of the Poles themselves – at the Tehran Conference in late 1943.

Churchill and Roosevelt, in line with their by now well-established policy of virtually unqualified conciliation of Stalin over East European matters, agreed in secret at that conference that the Soviet Union would be allowed to annex Poland's eastern provinces at the end of the war.[24] Churchill went through the motions of arguing then, and for a time afterwards, that Lwów should remain in Poland, but he had abandoned even that empty gesture well before Yalta. In fact, Yalta merely confirmed, in many ways, what had already been agreed about Poland by the 'Big Three' at Tehran. Moreover, major developments from that time until early 1945 ensured that this would be the case: the relentless advance of the Red Army on the Eastern Front, which brought it into pre-war Polish territory as early as January 1944; the decision of the Western Powers not to launch a military campaign from the Balkans aimed at bringing their forces into Central Europe ahead of the Soviets; and the failure of the Warsaw Rising by the underground Home Army (AK) in autumn 1944, which dealt a final, devastating blow to the already desperate political situation of the Polish government in London.

Informed observers could already see the writing on the wall as far as the Poles were concerned. Sir Cuthbert Headlam (1876–1964), a Conservative MP, remarked in the summer of 1944:

I am afraid that our Government may play the dirty on the decent Poles here ... To allow the Russians to set up a Bolshevik form of government in Poland and set up what frontier they like would be a pitiable thing to do, ruinous to our prestige in Europe.[25]

A few months later, he was in even more critical mood, insisting that 'what we are doing now is to make ourselves a partner in a new partition of Poland'.[26]

In reality, the Poles had been crushed well before Yalta by the military and diplomatic advance of the Soviet Union, and by the cynical disregard shown for them by their Western allies. Neither Churchill, despite his general sympathy for the Poles in the face of Stalin's intransigent animosity towards them, nor especially Roosevelt, had any real, sustained interest in the fate of Eastern Europe, for their main priorities lay elsewhere. They were also both haunted after 1941 by the thought of Stalin and Hitler joining up together again, this time to confront the West.[27] Determined to prevent such a nightmare scenario, they were prepared to appease

Stalin, even to the extent of sacrificing the interests of another ally, the Poles, whom they now facilely and opportunistically criticised for being politically unrealistic.[28]

At the same time, Churchill and Roosevelt constantly stressed the importance of perpetuating their wartime alliance with Stalin into the post-war era. They both had concluded that the rise of the Soviet Union as a world power was unstoppable, and that partnership with it, despite their obvious ideological differences, was the key to a post-war international order of peace and harmony. Besides, Roosevelt wanted the Soviets to enter the war against Japan. Underlining this approach was the encouragement given by the British and American governments to increasingly strident pro-Soviet propaganda in their countries, the purpose of which was simultaneously to put the London Poles in as unfavourable a light as possible. In Britain, the BBC, the Beaverbrook press and the Foreign Office, bastions of the Establishment, were especially culpable in this respect.[29]

From a different perspective, and one that is perhaps not usually appreciated by most Poles in Britain, the Poles themselves may be said to have contributed unwittingly to some degree to their diminishing image and final betrayal. The Polish government was rarely, if ever, united behind either Sikorski or his lesser successors, Stanisław Mikołajczyk (1900–66) and Tomasz Arciszewski (1877–1955), a situation that the Western Allies found more and more tiresome, especially as they came to regard the Poles as over-ambitious and politically naive.[30] The often fissiparous character of the Polish government was underlined by the fact that several of its senior ministers subsequently went over quickly and, it seems, without compunction, to the communist regime in Warsaw shortly after the end of the war. They included Henryk Strasburger (1887–1951), Ludwik Grosfeld and Jan Stańczyk (1886–1953), all of the Polish Socialist Party (PPS). The Poles, lacking the necessary resources, also failed to counter effectively the persistent, if fallacious, allegations of anti-Semitism in their ranks, especially in the army,[31] while their strong anti-Soviet outlook ran counter to the popular and official mood in the West during the last years of the war and for a while afterwards.

Some time before Yalta, therefore, the Poles had lost political credibility and influence. They had been marginalised by the power politics of the 'Big Three', who saw them as expendable. The outrage expressed by the Poles at the Yalta outcome was, however justified on moral grounds, not rooted in a realistic appraisal of political, diplomatic and military developments since at least 1943, and arguably since 1941. On the other hand, their warnings about Soviet intent after Yalta proved to be wholly accurate. In stark contrast to Churchill and Roosevelt, who had little knowledge of the Russians and their ways, the Poles, who had, of course, centuries of first-hand contact with their eastern neighbours, warned time and again that Stalin could not be trusted to keep his word, and that he would act as he saw fit to advance Soviet interests, whatever the implications for international agreements. Roosevelt, in particular, frequently comes across as a naive, ill-informed and unreliable judge of Stalin's character, intentions and actions. At the Tehran and Yalta conferences, he was overeager to please Stalin. His only real concern at the former conference appears to have been his own re-election prospects. His notoriously cynical remark to the Soviet leader encapsulates his approach:

> There are between six and seven million Americans of Polish extraction and I do not wish to lose their vote. Therefore, although I personally agree with your general view that Poland's frontiers should be moved to the West, I cannot publicly take part in any such arrangement at the present time, nor in the following winter.[32]

Contrary to Stalin's assurances about wanting a strong, independent Poland, to the USA's earlier reservations about the Lublin communists, and to the British view that the Soviet leader knew not to 'overreach' himself,[33] Polish warnings about Stalin were fully vindicated, in the first instance, by the nature of the Red Army's 'liberation' of Poland, which was characterised by wholesale murder, deportations, political trials and ruthless exploitation of material resources. Then, a determined campaign, backed by the Soviet secret police (NKVD) and its Polish communist counterpart (UB), was launched to establish the political hegemony of the Soviet-dominated Provisional Government of National Unity, and to transform Poland into a Soviet satellite.[34] Other political parties, such as the Polish Socialist Party and the Peasant Party, soon found themselves subjected to violent intimidation and harassment, with the aim of either scaring away their leaders and members or forcing them into compliance with the wishes of the communists, whose leaders were handpicked by the Soviets.[35] Many of them were not

Polish at all, but Russian, and some were even secret agents, like Bolesław Bierut (1892–1956), who assumed Polish names and were frequently of Jewish origin. These Jewish communists soon exercised a considerable degree of power in the most important branches of the embryonic state apparatus, the army, police, economy, education, the media and so on.[36] The 'free and unfettered' elections envisaged at Yalta never materialised. Instead, when they were eventually held, in January 1947, the anti-communist and anti-Soviet opposition had been largely eliminated, while, for good measure, the elections themselves were subject to wide-ranging irregularities that made a mockery of their proclaimed 'democratic' character.

This is not, of course, to overlook that in Poland immediately after 1945 there was a widespread desire, skilfully exploited by the communists, to rebuild the devastated country. Communism appeared to offer, in theory and on the surface, an appealing alternative to capitalism, which had often become associated in the popular mind in Poland with the misery of the Depression of the early 1930s, with fascism and, not least, with Western indifference to Poland's fate in 1945. Land reform, nationalisation and the reconstruction plan of 1945–47 enjoyed general support, and a *rapprochement* of sorts was effected for a time between the regime and the Catholic Church, particularly regarding policy in the so-called 'Recovered Territories' and towards the Church's property and schools.[37]

Not until the Moscow-based American diplomat George Kennan (1904–) produced in early 1946 a critical analysis of Soviet policy did the United States government, then led by President Harry Truman (1884–1972), begin to adopt a more hard-headed attitude towards the Soviet Union. Kennan convincingly argued that the country was expansionist on the basis of a revolutionary Marxist ideology.[38] About the same time, Churchill made his famous 'Iron Curtain' speech in Fulton, Missouri, and Stalin himself inadvertently gave weight to the fresh appraisal under way when, in early 1946, he menacingly affirmed the superiority of the Soviet system.[39] It was too late, however, to do anything about the situation in Poland, even if there had been the political will in Britain and the United States to do so, which there wasn't. In fact, the whole course of events in Poland since 1945 had been received with indifference, or, as in the case of the rigged elections, merely muted and ineffective protest. The pro-Soviet propaganda and attitudes of the war and early post-war period would require more time to wear off. At that juncture, with all the illusions about peace and harmony with the Soviets well and truly dispelled, Europe was about the enter the era of the Cold War.

Poland ended the war, therefore, as much the victim of Western apathy and cynicism as of Soviet imperialism, an outcome that was neither justified nor merited, despite the shortcomings and mistakes of the Polish government itself. Poland had simply not been important or powerful enough in the maelstrom of international power politics, leaving it open to the indignity of betrayal by those who were its putative friends and allies. The derecognised Polish government that remained in London after 1945 continued to repudiate the Yalta decisions on Poland and attracted support for some years from a few states, including the Vatican and the Irish Republic, and from several Conservative MPs, such as Sir Bernard Braine (1914–2000). Not until the election of Ronald Reagan (1911–) as US president in 1982, however, did its views resonate in any noticeable way in the international arena.[40]

A large majority of the 250,000 Poles in Britain in 1945–46 reluctantly decided that exile, even if temporary, was the only feasible option for them, particularly as many had now witnessed their homes in eastern Poland being swallowed up by the Soviet Union. They had to start thinking about a new life as civilians in a country that was now rather hostile to them at both an official and popular level.[41] The Establishment ensured that Yalta's significance for Poland was rarely mentioned in the public domain, just as was the case in communist Poland, while some important trade unions and large sections of the Labour Party regarded anti-Polish attitudes as the natural complement of their pro-Sovietism.

Most Polish veterans carried with them in those early post-war days two major and interconnected sources of consolation: the first was the understanding that the situation in communist Poland was infinitely worse than that in Britain, and the second was the belief, and indeed expectation, that a war would soon break out between the Western Powers and the Soviet Union, whereupon they would be recalled to the colours in a final drive to bring real liberation to their country. As the Cold War took root, however, such hopes were dashed. The Poles then had to decide, as permanent exiles, how far to maintain their Polishness and how far to assimilate into a country they really had not anticipated or wished to be part of.

Polish organisations of various types soon emerged, including the Polish Ex-Combatants' Association (SPK), parishes and churches, a press, cultural groups, commercial enterprises, language schools and so on.[42] Marriage with British women promoted integration perhaps more directly than anything else. However, if assimilation did take place where that first generation of Poles was concerned, it was perhaps frequently a somewhat superficial, grudging experience, for their hearts and souls remained strongly attached to the Poland they had been forced to leave behind and for which they had fought so courageously in battlefields across the whole of Europe. No doubt, a certain romantic nostalgia helped influence that outlook, but it was nevertheless genuine and wholesome.

Although in the Polish community that took shape in the early post-war years there was inevitably a small band of renegades, opportunists and communist sympathisers who made their accommodation with the Warsaw regime, the patriotic majority, guided by the Polish government-in-exile notwithstanding its isolated status and internecine wrangling, refused steadfastly to recognise its legitimacy and continued to repudiate Yalta altogether.[43] Instead, it cherished the hope that one day the regime would be overthrown and Yalta reversed. However, as time went on, this attitude may not have continued to be held by so many in the Polish community, since its character changed quite significantly. As the wartime generation grew fewer in number through natural causes, the Poles who subsequently came to this country – for example, following the major crises in Poland of 1956, 1968, 1970 and 1980–81 – did not necessarily subscribe to this uncompromising view of Yalta. They had been raised and educated, after all, in a highly sovietised communist system in which the truth about the war and its aftermath was usually distorted or suppressed. Nor, for that matter, and for quite different reasons, did many of the second and third generations of Poles born in Britain have intense feelings about Yalta. For one, they assimilated much more easily than their Polish parents and grandparents and looked to the future far more than to the past.

In any event, discussion in émigré circles in this country about Yalta and its consequences came to nothing until, of course, the events of 1989–90 in Poland, by which time most of the first Polish generation in Britain had passed away. Even then, however, change was only partial. Although the communist regime collapsed and Poland was re-established once more as an independent, sovereign country, and the Russians were soon on the way home, the eastern borders determined at Yalta remained, and indeed, were formally accepted by the first post-communist government in Poland. It can be said with absolute certainty that not everyone in the Polish community here is able or willing to accept that decision as final, even if the prospects of reversing Yalta in this regard hardly exist, either in a wider international context or within that of the present political situation in Poland itself.[44]

In a strange, ironic twist of fate, the national government in Poland, in respect of parliament, the Senate and the presidency, is currently dominated by 'former' communists, whose one-time ultimate allegiance to the Soviet Union and communism had ensured that Yalta became one of the infamous 'blank spots' in modern Polish history, a taboo subject.[45] All the more reason, therefore, for repudiating Yalta! Whatever the future holds – and it is perhaps worth recalling that national borders in Europe have been changed repeatedly over the centuries – there is no denying that Yalta, whether seen from the perspective of 1945 or from the present day, was for Poland one of the great iniquities of the twentieth century, and an appalling blot on the record of international diplomacy.

NOTES

1. K. Sword, with N. Davies and J. Ciechanowski, *The Formation of the Polish Community in Great Britain, 1939–1950* (London: School of Slavonic and East European Studies, 1989), pp. 17–18, 21–7.
2. The 'Curzon Line', initially put forward to the Allied Supreme Council in December 1919 by the British Foreign Secretary, Lord George Curzon, was suggested in July 1920 as the basis for determining the Polish–Russian border. The Polish government rejected the proposal outright, however, because it would have meant the surrender of much territory that was historically Polish.
3. S. Meiklejohn Terry, *Poland's Place in Europe; General Sikorski and the Origin of the Oder-Neisse Line, 1939–1943* (Princeton, NJ: Princeton University Press, 1983), pp. 245–314.
4. Polish Government in Exile, Z. C. Szkopiak (ed.), *The Yalta Agreements. Documents.* (London: Caldra House, 1986), pp. 23–9.
5. Ibid., p. xv.
6. Ibid., pp. 87–8. This was merely a restatement of the Soviet line since 1941, which was accepted at face value by, among others in Britain, the Foreign Secretary, Anthony Eden:see his letter of 4 July 1941 to Sir Stafford Cripps, British Ambassador in Moscow, in A. Polonsky (ed.), *The Great Powers and the Polish Question, 1941–1945* (London: Orbis Books, 1976), pp. 81–2, and Cripps to Eden of 6 December 1941, ibid., p. 95.
7. *The Yalta Agreements*, pp. 30–31. The Atlantic Charter, signed by Churchill and Roosevelt in August 1941, opposed territorial changes achieved by force and asserted the right of all nations to choose their own form of government.

8. Ibid., pp. 17–18.
9. Ibid., pp. 31–5.
10. Ibid., pp. 123–5.
11. Ibid., pp. 144–7. See the unconvincing article by A. M. Cienciała, 'Great Britain and Poland Before and After Yalta (1943–1945): A Reassessment', *Polish Review*, XL, 1995, no. 3, pp. 281–313.
12. This created another storm of protest. See letter of 6 July 1945 from the Polish Ambassador in London, Edward Raczyński, to the British government, and from the Polish Ambassador in Washington, Jan Ciechanowski, to the American government, also 6 July 1945, *The Yalta Agreements*, pp. 43–7.
13. Archive of the Centre for Research in Polish History (ACRPH), University of Stirling, A2, statement by B. Lewandowski (pseudonym), July 2000.
14. Background in M. K. Dziewanowski, *The Communist Party of Poland. An Outline of its History* (Cambridge, MA: Harvard University Press, 1976); J. Schatz, *The Generation. The Rise and Fall of the Jewish Communists of Poland* (Berkeley: University of California Press, 1991); J. B. de Weydenthal, *The Communists of Poland. An Historical Outline* (Stanford, CA: Hoover Institution Press, 1978).
15. *The Glasgow Herald*, 8 July 1940, p. 4. See also Chapter 5 of this volume.
16. R. Jenkins, *Churchill. A Biography* (London: Pan, 2002), pp. 761–3.
17. N. Davies, 'Lloyd George and Poland, 1919–20', *Journal of Contemporary History*, 6, 1971, no. 1, pp. 132–54.
18. P. S. Wandycz, *Polish Diplomacy, 1914–1945. Aims and Achievements* (London: Orbis Books, 1988), pp. 30ff.
19. For example, see speech by Lord Halifax in the House of Lords, 28 October 1939, in Polonsky, *Great Powers*, p. 74; and letter of 16 March 1940 from Sir William Strang to Sir Howard Kennard, ibid., p. 76.
20. J. Garliński, *Poland in the Second World War* (London: Macmillan, 1985), pp. 106ff. Details of the Pact in the Sikorski Historical Institute, *Documents on Polish–Soviet Relations, 1939–1945* (London: Heinemann, 1961), vol. I, pp. 141–2. See also A. M. Cienciała, 'General Sikorski and the Conclusion of the Polish-Soviet Agreement of July 30, 1941: A Reassessment', *Polish Review*, 41, 1996, no. 4, pp. 401–34.
21. A. M. Cienciała, 'The Polish Government's Policy on the Polish-Soviet Frontier in World War II as Viewed by American, British and Canadian Historians', *The Polish Review*, XLVI, 2001, no. 1, pp. 3–26.
22. K. Sword (ed.), *Sikorski. Soldier and Statesman* (London: Orbis Books, 1990), pp. 114–37.
23. Sikorski Historical Institute, *Documents*, vol. I, pp. 533–4.; see memorandum from Soviet minister Molotov to Polish minister Romer of 25 April 1943, in Polonsky, *Great Powers*, p. 126; A. J. Prażmowska, *Britain and Poland, 1939–1943. The Betrayed Ally* (Cambridge: Cambridge University Press, 1995), pp. 174f.
24. *The Yalta Agreements*, pp. 61–70; G. V. Kacewicz, *Great Britain, the Soviet Union and the Polish government-in-exile (1939–1945)* (The Hague: Martinus Nijhoff, 1979), pp. 164–82. Roosevelt had been hinting at this well before the conference: see his telegram of 16 March 1943 to Anthony Eden, in Polonsky, *Great Powers*, p. 118. For the wider context, see W. F. Kimball, *Forged in War. Roosevelt, Churchill and the Second World War* (London: HarperCollins, 1997).
25. S. Ball (ed.), *Parliament and Politics in the Age of Churchill and Atlee. The Headlam Diaries 1935–1951* (Cambridge: Cambridge University Press, 1999), p. 416, entry for 12 August 1944.
26. Ibid., p. 437, entry for 16 December 1944.

27. J. Karski, *The Great Powers and Poland, 1919–1945. From Versailles to Yalta* (New York: University Press of America,1985), pp. 451–67, 513–20, 559ff.
28. Letter from Eden to Churchill of 24 December 1943, in Polonsky, *Great Powers*, pp. 170–71.
29. M. Kitchen, *British Policy Towards the Soviet Union during the Second World War* (London: Croom Helm, 1986), pp. 100–3. Lord Beaverbrook, the press baron, was among the most outspoken admirers of the Soviet Union. See also D. Carlton, *Churchill and the Soviet Union* (Manchester: Manchester University Press, 1999), pp. 186–210; M. H. Folly, *Churchill, Whitehall and the Soviet Union, 1940–45* (London: HarperCollins, 2000) discusses shifting attitudes and intrigues in the 'corridors of power'.
30. Wandycz, *Polish Diplomacy*, p. 34.
31. D. Engel, *Facing a Holocaust. The Polish government-in-exile and the Jews, 1943–1945* (Chapel Hill: University of North Carolina Press, 1993), pp. 127–37.
32. *The Yalta Agreements*, p. xv. For the essential background, see R. C. Lukas, *The Strange Allies. The United States and Poland, 1941–1945* (Knoxville: University of Tennessee Press, 1978); W. F. Kimball, *The Juggler. Franklin Roosevelt as Wartime Statesman* (Princeton, NJ: Princeton University Press, 1991); R. H. Ferrell, *The Dying President* (Columbia, MO, 1998).
33. F. D. Roosevelt's *Briefing Papers, 1944–45*, 'Suggested United States Policy Regarding Poland', and Memorandum by J. Balfour to the Foreign Office, 12 March 1945 (my thanks to Madeleine C. Stachura for providing these documents, December 2001).
34. J. W. Young, *Cold War Europe, 1945–1989* (London: Edward Arnold, 1991), p. 3.
35. N. Davies, *God's Playground. A History of Poland. Volume II* (Oxford: Clarendon Press, 1981), pp. 548–9, 556–60, 565–70; S. Mikołaczyk, *The Rape of Poland. Pattern of Soviet Aggression* (New York: Whittlesey House, 1948), pp. 203–42.
36. S. Korboński, *The Jews and the Poles in World War II* (New York: Hippocrene Press, 1989), pp. 73–87; Peter D. Stachura, 'Polish–Jewish Relations in the Aftermath of the Holocaust: Reflections and Perspectives', in P. D. Stachura (ed.), *Perspectives on Polish History* (Stirling: Centre for Research in Polish History, University of Stirling, 2001), pp. 88–9. See also the Extracts of Minutes of the PPR (Polish Communist Party) Central Committee Meeting, 20–21 May 1945, Document 75, in A. Polonsky and B. Drukier, *The Beginnings of Communist Rule in Poland, December 1943–June 1945* (London: Routledge & Kegan Paul, 1980), pp. 424–43. Further details are in Documents 76–79, ibid., pp. 444–49.
37. G. Roberts, *The Soviet Union in World Politics: Coexistence, Revolution and Cold War, 1945–1991* (London: Macmillan, 1999), pp. 27ff.
38. K. Kersten, *The Establishment of Communist Rule in Poland, 1943–1948* (Berkeley: University of California Press, 1991), pp. 285–341; C. Kennedy-Pipe, *Stalin's Cold War. Soviet Strategies in Europe, 1943 to 1956* (Manchester: Manchester University Press, 1985), pp. 45–66; J. Rothschild, *Return to Diversity. A Political History of East Central Europe Since World War II* (Oxford: Oxford University Press, 1993), pp. 79–89.
39. Stalin speech, 9 February 1946, published in *Soviet News*.
40. *The Yalta Agreements*, pp. 152–78; on Braine, see obituary in the *Polish Society Newsletter*, no. 9, Winter 1999–2000, p. 2.
41. *House of Commons Debates*, Fifth Series, vol. 423, col. 2233, MP's anti-Polish statement of 6 June 1946, and ibid., vol. 431, col. 53, reference of 3 December 1946.
42. ACRPH, *The Thornton Private Papers*, memorandum of 14 February 1949 from

the Catholic Council of Polish Welfare; Sword *et al.*, *Formation of the Polish Community*, pp. 357–457.

43. K. Sword, *Identity in Flux. The Polish Community in Britain* (London: School of Slavonic and East European Studies, 1996), pp. 22–58.
44. For example, among members of the Polish Society, based in Scotland: see its *Newsletter*, no. 9, Winter 1999–2000, p. 2.
45. See G. C. Malcher, *Blank Pages. Soviet Genocide against the Polish People* (Woking: Pyrford Press, 1993).

3

The Establishment
of the Polish Section
of the SOE

Jeffrey Bines

On 26 July 1939, a Major of the Polish Intelligence Corps addressed a group of British Military Intelligence officers assembled in the resident clerk's office, next to room 427 of the War Office, in London. The subject of his talk was plans for guerrilla-style warfare to be carried out should the Germans invade and overrun Poland. Late in August, a Military Mission, the Number 4 Military Mission, was despatched to Poland by the British Government to carry out two tasks. The first of these was to keep the War Office in London 'fully and continuously' informed of the military situation, and the second was to ensure a continuation programme for cooperation by the Polish Army in the combined plan of the Allies. Added to the brief was a note urging the Mission, in view of the difficulties involved in supplying direct support to the Poles, to do everything, as a matter of the greatest importance, to inspire confidence.[1]

Chief of Staff to the leader of the Mission was Lt.-Col. Colin Gubbins, an intelligence officer. He left England with a number of regular and reserve officers and personnel from the Royal Corps of Signals, and met the Mission's leader, Major General Adrian Carton de Wiart, who was already in Warsaw. Gubbins and his party arrived on 3 September, the very day that Britain declared war on Germany. The Military Mission contacted and remained with Marshal Edward Śmigły-Rydz, the Polish Commander-in-Chief, and his staff through-out the September campaign, offering advice and assistance when-ever possible. Ultimately, Poland fell and the Marshal reluctantly retreated into a still friendly Romania whilst the opportunity existed. Led by Gubbins, the British Military Mission followed.

General Carton de Wiart was later to write:

> The Polish Army fought to the last gasp; my action in this sphere was confined to pressing the Polish Chief of Staff to adopt a sound strategy. It only remained for me to keep the War Office fully informed of the military situation ... and to study the strategical and tactical lessons of the fighting: this I was able to do by the efforts of my staff and my signals personnel.[2]

Among those commended in his report were the names of three men who would become important to the Polish Section: Lt.-Col. Colin Gubbins, (Acting Captain) Peter Wilkinson and (Acting Captain) Harold Perkins.

Initially, one of the major tasks was to placate the attitude of Britain's recently (if only temporarily) defeated ally – the Polish people. In his report of the mission, Captain Tommy Davies stated:

> General Carton de Wiart wished me to say that the delay of 48 hours of the British declaration of war had caused the greatest mistrust of our intentions and this will continue to exist until positive action is taken by the British forces to relieve pressure on the Eastern frontier.

Assistance from Britain and France had been expected by the Poles from the outset of hostilities, and it was not only the Polish General Staff officers who had wondered where support from the French and British air forces was. Troops on the ground looked up in anticipation that friendly aircraft would soon be overhead. The reason that they were not was simple: the Allies hardly possessed an aeroplane with the range to fly to Poland, let alone fight once there. Memos flew back and forth between Air Commodore Medhurst, the Director of Allied Air Cooperation, and the various departments concerned. If the bombers could have flown as well as the memos, perhaps more could have been done, for it certainly was not through lack of trying. The reality was that bombers of the period could carry sufficient fuel to make a one-way trip, but that was about all. They could not land and refuel for the return because, from the start of the German invasion, virtually all the aerodromes on Polish soil had been overrun and were in the hands of the enemy. The possibility of aid from Allied ground forces at the time was, of course, non-existent.

Only those in Poland who had already been overrun, including the members of the British Mission, knew the effect of blitzkrieg, which surely was soon to be unleashed in the West. During what became known as the 'phoney war', there was time for a number of lessons to be learned by those whose job it was to learn them. Gubbins was more than sensible to the danger and, as in his report of 20 May 1939 in which he stated in a message to his immediate superior that he had had no doubt that the Poles would fight, he now accurately predicted that: '... this autumn or next spring we shall be faced in the West with the forces which the Poles have had to contend so courageously but so hopelessly [with]. We must go absolutely nap on anti-tank guns, and light anti-aircraft (guns) for the forward areas'.[3]

That Poland had recognised the possibility of being overrun is evident in the manner in which plans had been laid for an underground army. Time would prove that no other nation in the war, either occupied or soon to be occupied, operated such a well-organised force so effectively, or for so long. In some British circles, this potential was already recognised. Douglas Dodds-Parker, an intelligence officer, wrote a letter in which he stressed the importance of assisting the Poles as much as possible. 'Underground organisations will become most effective,' it said: 'They should always feel they have the greatest support from us and not feel obligation.'[4]

The British Military Attaché in Rome wrote to Major-General Beaumont-Nesbitt, the Director of Military Intelligence (MI), informing him that large numbers of arms had been hidden in Poland for the use of small groups currently attacking the Russians. He considered this a pointless act at that time, no doubt believing it a waste of valuable manpower that could be better utilised at a later date. He was correct, for within days Colonel Kedzior, the Polish Chief of Staff, contacted Gubbins to say that the situation in Poland was becoming desperate. By now, the Polish General Staff had established its headquarters in Paris, liaising directly with the French General Staff. At the same time, a branch of the Polish Second Bureau (Intelligence) began to establish courier lines in and out of Poland, and to plan for and develop the resistance organisations within the country.

In Paris, liaison links between the Poles and the British had only been available through the French authorities. Against strong French opposition, the British sought to establish direct liaison links with the Poles, which, once set up, gave Gubbins the authority he needed to work with them to investigate the possibility of British involvement in their clandestine operations. It became apparent, however, that decisions, especially those of the British, could only be made after consultation with the highest authorities.

On 27 November, in a move that was probably intended to keep the peace with the French, the British Military Mission, by now much reduced in size, formally established itself in Paris under the title of the Number 2 Liaison Mission.[5] Gubbins headed a team of four: himself, Captain Lloyd-Johnes and a secretary as permanent members, with Captain Wilkinson remaining in his Military Intelligence role as 'Rear Link' in London. Gubbins's plan was to control all guerrilla activities abroad from one central office with a bureau for each country section situated in London. These bureaux would be controlled by the British General Staff, but with the right of appeal via the representatives of the respective governments. The Polish leader, General Sikorski, was keen on the idea and appeared anxious to see Gubbins to discuss it. It was abundantly clear, though, that any guerrilla actions could not yet be carried out successfully and that a great deal of organising had first to be done. Of prime importance was the supply of communications equipment in order to establish links with representatives abroad.

During December 1939, Lt.-Col. Gano, of Polish Intelligence, returned from a reconnaissance trip to Budapest, Belgrade and Bucharest, where he had set up intelligence network bases. He was advised by the British to increase his lines of communications and to stop all subversive action within Poland for the time being. This, it was thought, would give everyone a chance to reorganise and prepare to take delivery of more equipment intended for later and more effective use. At the beginning of 1940, Gubbins and his team, now reconstituted as the Number 4 Military Mission, took responsibility for assisting the Poles in the organisation of these infiltration routes to the above cities, at which points the Poles took over the onward transportation of couriers and equipment.

General Kazimierz Sosnkowski, of the Polish High Command, reported that Polish guerrilla leaders were established in previously allotted districts and were anticipating being supplied by either the British or the French. Within a short time, stores were being delivered by the British, and up until 1 April 1940, wireless telephony sets, revolvers, ammunition, high explosive and incendiary devices were already in Polish hands. Unfortunately, fears previously expressed by the British Mission regarding the security of lines of supply were being realised. It was now much more difficult to get equipment through Romania, due to tighter border controls.

On 1 April, Gubbins was detached from the Mission in Paris for service in Norway. Captain Dodds-Parker joined the Mission but remained based in London in place of Wilkinson, who had taken command of the Mission in Gubbins's place. Also rejoining was Captain Harold Perkins, the member from the 1939 mission. Known affectionately as Perks, he would later take responsibility for the entire Polish section.

The British Liaison Mission remained in Paris until 10 June, at which time it followed the Polish General Staff as it moved, first to Angers, and later to Bordeaux. Italy's declaration of war on Britain and France probably troubled them little, but the news that the Germans were within 35 miles of Paris certainly would have occupied their thoughts. It was obvious that France could not maintain any sort of defensive stance against the onrushing Germans, so on 15 June Wilkinson returned to Britain temporarily to arrange preparations for the arrival of the Polish Army in the United Kingdom. Two days later, Lloyd-Johnes and Richard Truszkowski, a British officer of Polish descent, contacted the Polish HQ and tried to make hurried arrangements for the evacuation of the Polish personnel. The following day, the Mission was ordered to return to the UK.

Wilkinson, in the meantime, had returned to France and made contact with General Sikorski, accompanying and assisting him in making arrangements for the evacuation of the Polish troops. The day after the Mission was ordered back, Wilkinson again returned to England, this time with Sikorski and twelve other high-ranking Polish staff officers. They were the first members of the Polish Army to arrive in Britain, but the arrival went relatively unnoticed by the public as it was also the day that Britain welcomed the first Australian and New Zealand troops.

Upon his arrival in Britain, Sikorski assured everyone that he intended to continue to fight against the Germans, but only under certain conditions. The first of these was that he should be granted the full rights and privileges of a government. The British concurred, but it was a clear indication that from that moment onwards the Poles intended to determine their own destiny as much as they could. They would henceforth retain total control over their communications in all aspects of the clandestine war that they were waging in their homeland. This was not altogether to the liking of some departments of the British Foreign Office, in particular the Secret Intelligence Service (SIS), who preferred to keep their finger on all pulses. Nevertheless, it was agreed.

The Poles soon began to establish themselves in England and Scotland, initially under an area commander. Eventually, the Polish Army in Britain came under the control of Joint Allied Staff, and sense dictated that this should be so. The rapidly emerging underground army in Poland would remain under the strict control of the Polish government, which came to consider its underground army as the most important of its forces. The British administration recognised a valuable ally and showed great sensitivity in not questioning Poland's right to determine her own home politics and control of her people.

The Polish government and General Staff were soon firmly established in London, where they gradually assumed greater importance. Morale was reported to be high amongst the Polish troops stationed in Glasgow. Indeed, they had all expressed great satisfaction at being there and generally considered themselves well treated. On the other hand, they complained with bitterness about the way they felt the French had let them down, and spoke of hindrance and opposition by the French towards their evacuation. It was noted, though, and not surprisingly, that there was a certain amount of indiscipline amongst the Poles, due to the fact that they were made up of many different units. In some cases they had lost their officers and were disorganised. The British thought this perfectly understandable and were encouraged to hear that both the military authorities and the local inhabitants of the Glasgow area had expressed their satisfaction with the Poles' behaviour and considered them better than other foreign troops who had been stationed there.

By now, Glasgow was home to around 12,500 troops, including 2,000 officers. All of them had rifles of mixed sorts, mainly French in design and manufacture. Some had brought with them a few mortars as well as anti-tank guns and rifles, and about 20–30 machine guns. They also had one lorry, three tractors and 112 mules! The mules were quickly found pastures new and put to use elsewhere. Security, however, was a problem as there were many civilians mixed with the troops who had also been evacuated from the continent. These civilians, it was thought likely, could include a few German spies. The troops couldn't vouch for these people. Indeed, with such a mixture of units and companies, most of the time they couldn't even vouch for one another. So it was decided that identities would be sorted out once more permanent camps had been allotted.

It was wisely recognised at this time that the Poles had considerable experience in fighting the Germans, more so, in fact, than anyone else. As well as the September campaign, they had featured prominently during the French and Norwegian campaigns, and fighting on all fronts was a trend they would continue until the end of the war. It was therefore proposed that priority for re-equipping would be given to the Poles in preference to British raw recruits.

At the end of June 1940, Perkins paid a visit to 11 Park Street, Glasgow, to meet those responsible for assisting the Poles to settle in. In the meantime, some reorganisation was going on in London amongst the British, and from now onwards the Poles concerned with clandestine operations worked with a newly formed branch of the Military Mission, under the control of a Brigadier Bridge. Wilkinson discovered that the Poles, too, were reorganising and had created a new department under the Polish General Staff, called the Sixth Bureau, to deal with subversive action within Poland. The former Chief of Polish Intelligence, Józef Smolenski, headed the new bureau.

Lt.-Col. Gano informed Colonel Jo Holland, of British Military Intelligence section MIR, that General Sikorski wanted the new Sixth Bureau and the Polish Intelligence Service (Second Bureau) to be closely bound with their British counterparts. After some thought, it was decided that the Second Bureau should be put directly in touch with MI6. Peter Wilkinson, anticipating the request, had previously spoken to an MI6 officer who was keen on the idea, and arrangements were made for Gano to contact this officer directly in future. Despite this 'defection' of the Polish Second Bureau to the SIS, close ties still continued between it and members of the Mission.

These reorganisations called for new thinking, but application of the long-term policy was already well advanced with the placement of the representatives in the neutral countries bordering Poland, and the establishment of supply lines to Poland that were being set up, through stores, in Alexandria. By now, Dodds-Parker was in Cairo reorganising communications, so it was suggested that he handled things at the Egyptian end, liaising with Perkins in London.[6] In the short term, plans were considered to attempt to halt the transportation of foodstuffs, goods and raw materials passing from Poland to Germany. Action would soon need to be taken to cause disruption to these lines of supply, perhaps with the aid of MIR specialities, the so-called 'dirty tricks'. The basic policy of MIR remained unchanged though, which was to assist the Polish organisation in active operations in Central Europe, to help maintain open lines of communication and, finally, to assist in the actual transportation of agents and equipment from this country to their fields of operation.

In early August 1940, Brigadier Bridge sent a letter from his room in London's Clifton Hotel to Major-General Beaumont-Nesbitt. It was considered important at the time and especially so at the end of the war, as it contained proposals that were subsequently adopted. Perhaps the most informative part of the letter was:

> There exists in Poland an active organisation controlled from London by Colonel Smolenski. The plan will be to send to Poland, by night, Polish parachutists with the special W/T Transceiver sets. These parachutists will land in a neighbourhood in which the Polish organisation is constantly on the watch and in which a signal system has been prepared and is already in operation … Such contact will ensure much closer cooperation than at present between the Polish VIth Bureau and their organisation in Poland and will ensure also the regular control of supplies, money, etc., as the need arises. There is no inherent impossibility in the plan from the flying point of view, and the Polish VIth Bureau is anxious that the necessary preparations shall be commenced with the least possible delay. I should, therefore, be glad if you could ask the Director of Military Training to make the necessary arrangements for the training of the W/T operators and parachutists.[7]

Once a set-up of long-range wireless telephony stations was underway, the next move was to train the potential Polish wireless operators on new transceiver sets at a special training centre at Lochailort, Scotland. On 12 August, news was passed that the first 50 Poles were ready to begin training immediately.[8] A message was sent to the Polish General Staff informing it that Captain Strawiński, as commander of a special unit, would be ready, with an interpreter, at his base in Glasgow to report to Lochailort at two hours' notice. Training was to cover almost all aspects of guerrilla fighting, despite the fact that this initial course was to last only nine days.

Until now, progress had generally been slow from both the Polish and the British sides of the equation. The groundwork had been done, however, and quite thoroughly, and this led to better understanding of each other's problems in the coming years. The understanding of the heads of various departments and their staff to their opposite numbers, and the cooperation throughout, was remarkable, and it ably demonstrated what could be achieved with the existence of the mutual respect that the organisations obviously had for each other. The settling-in period was drawing to a close. The first agents, described by Major Stacey, the Commanding Officer at the Lochailort Training Centre, to be as keen as mustard and the best he had there, were ready to take their places in the field.

On 26 September, Desmond Morton, Winston Churchill's Security Executive, sent a message to Hugh Dalton, the Minister of Economic Warfare, and consequently responsible for the Special Operations Executive (SOE). Morton had seen Colonel Mitkiewicz, the Polish Director of Military Intelligence, who controlled, with one exception, all naval, military and air intelligence, as well as the Secret Service for the Polish government. The one exception was an organisation run by Stanisław Kot, the Polish Minister for the Interior. Politically, Kot was a member of the Polish Peasant Party and had a reputation for being more than 'averagely Polish' for intrigue against his colleagues. He had been charged by Sikorski to control all subversive and underground civil activities within Poland itself. Morton suggested that Dalton should get directly in touch with Kot. Two days only went by before Dalton and Kot lunched together. Dalton promised help, as Kot outlined what he envisaged as his future requirements, one of which, significantly, was the return of Colonel Gubbins as liaison officer.

With the likelihood of the first parachute drop into Poland looming large on the horizon, contact between Kot and the newly returned Gubbins increased. In order that closer and more efficient liaison could be continued, a new, regular department was set up to deal with the Poles' problems. This was to be the Polish section of SO2, the operational branch of the SOE. It is probably safe to say that the Polish country section of the SOE was born during the third

week of November 1940. Sensibly, the section was staffed by virtually
the same MIR personnel as the previous Number 4 Mission, but they
now became the sole link with the Polish authorities concerned with
clandestine and underground actions, both in the Polish homeland
and elsewhere abroad.

Work would henceforth be done in closer collaboration with the
Polish Sixth Bureau. Through the SOE, exchanges of information
from other European countries fighting the clandestine war could
now be easily passed between the sections. All could then benefit
from common knowledge and intelligence. Gubbins became Director
of Training and Operations, with Wilkinson and Perkins joining
him. Until this time, the subversive resistance movements in Poland
had been under the guardianship of the War Office. From now on,
the Poles would, and to a greater extent than any other section of
SOE, control their own destiny. Control of agents in the field
would be solely the responsibility of the Polish government in
London. No other section of SOE enjoyed such autonomy. Dalton
was aware that he had been largely responsible for Gubbins's
posting to what, in military terms, was likely to be considered a back-
water. He had no intention of being responsible for causing
Gubbins's career to suffer and so, at the minister's insistence, he was
promoted Brigadier.

Much time was taken up with preparation and training for future
operations and, although the planned operations were intended to
be purely military, the political Poles, Kot's organisation, recognised
the possibility that they, too, might benefit from airborne operations.
Subsequently, they showed great interest, and to some relief on the
part of the British, the first indications of cooperation between the
political and military Poles slowly became evident. Perkins was in
daily contact with the Sixth Bureau and remained so. Smolenski
informed Perkins where he wanted the parachutists landed, and
asked him to let him have a decision on how soon it would be
possible for the first landing to take place.

On 20 December, the first flight to Poland to drop agents was
scheduled. The aircraft requirements had been laid out by the Sixth
Bureau long before. An aeroplane with the endurance for the 2,000-
mile round trip, having a speed of between 200 and 250 knots, would
be required to complete the journey within the hours of darkness,
in order to give the crew the best possible chance of survival. On the
actual day, the aircraft supplied by the RAF turned out to be a

Whitley that had a maximum range of only 750 miles, at a top speed of 130 knots! Not surprisingly, everyone was left wondering what the RAF was thinking about and whether it had even the remotest grasp of what was needed to accomplish the mission. It was apparently obvious it hadn't, and the flight was immediately cancelled.[9] Whether the fault lay entirely with the RAF or with the Polish Air Force liaison was difficult to determine. In an attempt to ensure that it would not happen again, if the fault had indeed been a Polish one, Colonel Smolenski informed Harold Perkins that, for future operations, he had taken the matter completely out of the hands of the Polish Air Force.[10]

Christmas was rapidly approaching, and Sikorski invited Minister Dalton and Brigadier Gubbins to join him in Scotland to celebrate the festivities. They flew from London to Perth on 23 December. Dalton was particularly impressed and found the time spent with Sikorski and his troops to be a moving experience. He retained a special affection for the Poles from that moment on.[11]

On the night of 15/16 February 1941, the first flight to Poland took place to deliver agents.[12] It was the first time that an agent had been parachuted by SOE anywhere into occupied Europe. An especially adapted Whitley, reaching a point 850 miles distant, carried out the operation, code-named Adolphus, and took 11 hours, 45 minutes, practically all of which was over enemy territory. On the basis of their experience, the Air Ministry decided that no further flights would be undertaken to Poland using Whitleys, and more suitable aircraft would have to be found. This flight was a record for a Whitley and only possible because of exceptionally favourable circumstances and meteorological conditions on the night.

Before departure, the agents were given miraculously produced letters from their families, which they read but were not allowed to take aboard the aircraft. The plane took off from Stradishall at 18.35 hours to fly to a point in the Kraków area. On the way, the men were kept occupied replying to their letters, having asked the crew to forward the replies to Poland on their return to England. The aircraft encountered anti-aircraft fire over Holland and searchlights over Germany in the Düsseldorf area, but the flight was otherwise uneventful. Near Breslau, it ran into heavy cloud and had to continue using dead reckoning. This brought it well south of the intended drop zone. It turned north and flew as near to the drop zone as fuel would allow. Exit from the Whitley was difficult and each man had to kneel in the doorway and literally be kicked out by the corporal dispatcher. The agents parachuted first, then the aircraft circled, remaining close to the drop zone; the containers followed. The rear gunner reported the containers all fell within a reasonable distance of the parachutists (the containers were never recovered). The actual place of arrival was Skoczów, some 80 miles from the intended place. The aircraft returned to Stradishall and landed at 06.05 hours. One of Kot's political couriers and two of the Sixth Bureau's secret agents, the first of the *Cichociemni* (the silent and unseen ones), had returned to Poland. The first delivery of agents signalled the end of the preparations for resistance, and the Polish section of SOE was finally in business. By the end of the war, 318 military (including one woman and one Hungarian) and 28 political couriers were parachuted into Poland by the Polish Section of SOE.[13]

NOTES

1. Public Record Office (PRO) Kew, file ref. HS4/223.
2. Ibid.
3. PRO Kew, file ref. HS4/224.
4. PRO Kew, file ref. HS4/178.
5. P. Wilkinson and J. Bright Astley, *Gubbins and SOE* (London: Pen and Sword, 1993), p. 48.
6. D. Dodds-Parker, *Setting Europe Ablaze* (Windlesham: Springfield Books, 1984), p. 44.
7. PRO Kew, file ref. HS4/184.
8. Ibid.
9. Ibid.
10. PRO Kew, ref. HS4/194.
11. PRO Kew ref. HS4/315 and HS4/149.
12. PRO Kew, ref. HS7/184.
13. J. Garliński, *Poland, SOE and the Allies* (London: Macmillan, 1969), pp. 235–8.

4

The Government of the Republic of Poland in Exile, 1945–92

Wojciech Rojek

After the lost military campaign in September 1939, the Polish govern-ment went into exile in Romania, where, contrary to assurances, it was interned. Consequently, President Ignacy Mościcki, acting according to the April 1935 Constitution, appointed Władysław Raczkiewicz his successor on 29 September. A day later, Raczkiewicz appointed General Władysław Sikorski as Prime Minister, and the following day heard the oath of the new cabinet members.

The government's political support during the war came from four parties: the Peasants' Party (PSL), National Party (SN), Polish Socialist Party (PPS) and Labour Party (SP). The cabinet resided in Paris until November 1939, then in Angers until June 1940, ending up in London for the rest of the war. Following Sikorski's death on 4 July 1943, Stanisław Mikołajczyk (PSL) became Prime Minister from 14 July 1943 until 24 November 1944, when he was succeeded by Tomasz Arciszewski (PPS). Throughout the war, the National Council of the Republic of Poland[1] played an advisory role to the government, whose situation became inordinately complicated when, on 29 June 1945, France, followed on 5 July by Britain and the United States, withdrew their recognition of it.[2] Still, this unrecognised government commanded the Polish Armed Forces, numbering 228,000 officers and men. Since the British had also stopped recognising the Commander-in-Chief, General Tadeusz Komorowski, they chose to deal with the Chief of Staff, General Stanisław Kopański, and Second Polish Corps commander, General Władysław Anders. Repatriation to Poland was sluggish. By spring

1946, only 6,800 soldiers had volunteered to return, while the rest were estimated at 160,000. On 21 May, Foreign Secretary Ernest Bevin presented to the Polish generals a plan to bring the Second Polish Corps to England and transform it into the Polish Resettlement Corps[3].

President Raczkiewicz's health declined suddenly in December 1946. Since his chosen successor, Arciszewski, was suffering a severe setback in influence, in April 1947 Raczkiewicz appointed August Zaleski instead. The latter had made a name for his staunch opposition to any compromise with the Soviet Union. Raczkiewicz died two months later and, on 9 June 1947, Zaleski was sworn in as President of Poland. The June crisis gave rise to political divisions among the Polish community abroad that would continue for years. The most active opposition group was the PPS. On 30 June, a Democratic Concentration was created. It included representatives of the PPS, the Polish Freedom Movement for Independence and Democracy, the Democratic Party and some from the SP.[4]

Arciszewski resigned on 2 July, and General Komorowski became Prime Minister. His chief objective was to regain the support of the PPS and other members of the Democratic Concentration. On 21 October, Mikołajczyk escaped from Poland, and after a brief stay in London, where his talks with Prime Minister Komorowski failed, he left for the United States, where he was given a hero's welcome by the highest authorities, including President Harry Truman. When, on 15 December 1947, an agreement was made between the Peasants' Party and the Polish-American Congress, it ignored the existence of the government of Poland in London.[5]

Attempts made until March 1948 to draw the PPS into the government failed. This meant a split in the Democratic Concentration and prevented a National Council and National Treasury being created. For his part, Mikołajczyk would not renounce his political ambitions. In May 1948, he became chairman of the International Peasants' Union, embracing representatives from central and south-eastern Europe. In summer, he visited London, and although his talks failed to result in the creation of a Polish National Committee, they did produce, on 15 November 1948, an Alliance of Democratic Parties (Peasants, Socialists, some Labour) that supported him. At that time, the American government favoured the idea of creating in the United States a committee to unite all the major forces on the Polish expatriate political scene.[6]

Meanwhile, the National Party under Tadeusz Bielecki was involved in a complicated scheme to ensure the political domination of the Polish community abroad by 'London Poles'. On 7 April 1949, Tadeusz Tomaszewski was appointed Prime Minister, which resulted in his expulsion from the PPS. He turned his back on the political parties and sought support from community organizations. He appointed members to another National Council. Also, the idea of a National Treasury finally took shape. Seventy per cent of its receipts were to cover the government's current expenditure, with the remainder set aside as a reserve. The National Council selected twelve members of its Chief Commission in December 1949.[7] The formation of the Tomaszewski cabinet drove the traditional political parties into opposition. In response, a new body, the Political Council, was created in December 1949, chaired by Arciszewski. In February 1950, it opened a New York office headed by Stefan Korboński.[8]

Efforts were made also to unite all groups of the Polish diaspora. In 1950, two unsuccessful attempts were made by General Anders and Professor Henryk Paszkiewicz. A year later, Generals Kazimierz Sosnkowski and Marian Kukiel also tried and failed to reconcile the many estranged factions of legalist circles on the basis of compromise.[9] In early 1953, Sosnkowski embarked on a new mediatory mission, and finally in June was able to submit to President Zaleski a proposed Unity Act. It stipulated that a future Poland, a democracy implementing social justice, should embrace territory from the borders drawn in the Treaty of Riga (1921) in the east to the Oder-Neisse line in the west. Detailed provisions spoke of a Council of National Unity to substitute for both legislative houses. By March 1954, the Unity Act had been recognized by all major political groups.[10]

With President Zaleski steadfastly hostile to unification, however, a break-up soon followed. Most politicians, despairing of the President's attitude, created a Provisional Council of National Unity (PCNU), leaving out those of its members who were to be appointed by the President under the failed Unity Act. The PCNU was to represent political parties and community organizations. On its inauguration in London on 31 July 1954, it appointed a Council of Three that would temporarily 'watch over the vital interests of the Republic', and appoint and discharge an Executive of National Unity. On 8 August, Tadeusz Bielecki was elected chairman of the

PCNU, and the Council of Three was composed of Arciszewski, Anders and Edward Raczyński. On 27 August, the Council named a quasi-government – the Executive of National Unity – with General Roman Odzierzyński as chairman.[11]

An opportunity for both groups to test their strength came with elections for the Council of the Republic in November 1954. However, only 4,661 voters turned up, out of a total of about 119,000 Poles then residing in Britain, of whom an estimated 33,500 were politically active. The Council sat for the first time in December, while the Chief Commission of the National Treasury, connected with the 'palace' (the President's circle), convened in January 1955. Even though many of the institution's old structures chose to back Zaleski, its financial situation was so bad that funding had to be sought in the United States.[12]

A serious crisis then shook the 'palace'. In July 1955, following the resignation of Stanisław Mackiewicz as Prime Minister, Zaleski appointed Hugo Hanke to replace him. Hanke arrived in Rome on 5 September seeking an audience with the Pope, but suddenly disappeared and five days later Warsaw announced his return to Poland. Hanke turned out to be an agent of Polish State Security.[13] This affair was the final blow to any swift compromise between the two estranged factions of the Polish independence-oriented emigration. In November 1955, in Manchester, about seven thousand Poles demonstrated in support of unity based on national and religious values, while renouncing any contacts with the Warsaw regime. By the end of 1955, a basic territorial structure of the PCNU had been built, with chapters in France, Canada and the United States.[14]

In the unity camp, meanwhile, it was debated whether to bestow the constitutional prerogatives of the President on the Council of Three. This was firmly opposed by General Sosnkowski, who argued that such a step would undermine the position of the Polish émigré government in the eyes of the world as there would be two parallel presidencies and two separate governments. A last attempt to prevent the break-up of the emigration into rival camps was made in April 1956 by Archbishop Józef Gawlina, but President Zaleski refused to back down one inch. As a result, in July 1956, the PCNU resolved, firstly, that the Council of Three was a senior body watching over vital interests and was to act vicariously as the President of the Republic of Poland, although it was not authorized to nominate a presidential successor; secondly, the Executive of National Unity was to act vicariously as Poland's government-in-exile. This was the final step in the creation of a legalist centre grounded in the Unity Act. It was also then that a new, decisive line of political division was drawn. The Council of Three was a kind of regency appointed by a parliamentary body. It controlled the emigration's political life through the Executive. In this arrangement, the PCNU was the source of other powers. This naturally raised the question of member mandates. Members of political parties claimed mandates won in pre-war elections or in the Polish underground. By contrast, activists involved with émigré community organizations preferred elections as the source of legitimacy. This was the fundamental difference.[15]

Mikołajczyk continued his efforts to hold sway over the Polish emigration, but faced a difficult situation with the creation of the Political Council, which, despite predictions, stood the test of time. Thus, any attempt to create a national committee that would include not only his own party but also other significant groups was seriously hampered. Yet efforts continued. In May 1950, the Polish Democratic Alliance (PDA) stated that it represented a clear majority of society, and that temporary systemic principles needed to be developed in the spirit of the 1921 Constitution, since that from 1935 had been forcibly imposed on the nation. In territorial matters, it favoured the Oder-Neisse line, while simultaneously rejecting the 1939 partition of Poland. The PDA further created a Polish National Democratic Committee (PNDC), which was a kind of controlling political body.[16] The authority of the Political Council, however, prevented the PNDC from being recognised, despite the vigorous support of the Americans, as a representative of the Polish *raison d'état*. The first clash was occasioned by the Liberty Declaration, prepared by Polish-American circles. In Philadelphia, in February 1951, the declaration was signed only by the PNDC. Consequently, in April Mikołajczyk could join the Committee for Central Europe, created in Washington. The PSL clearly predominated in the PNDC, other groups having merely symbolic significance.[17]

The riots in Poland in October 1956 led to disagreement among unification camp activists. One group distanced itself from the changes underway in Poland, maintaining that the emigration's principal political tenets – full independence and restitution of Poland's eastern border as defined in the Treaty of Riga – must not be altered. Committed to legitimacy as the legal and ideological basis for émigré life, it earned the nickname of 'Die-Hards'. The other faction concluded that Polish realities had changed sufficiently to call for a redefining of the political goals of the emigration. This led it to believe that short-term aims were more realistic in an evolving situation, and also on the international scene, and were thus called 'Realists'. They viewed legalism, so valued by the 'Die-Hards', as an anachronism. The formal émigré élites were to become a representation and to seek a mandate in elections.[18]

While the October events in Poland brought deep divisions in the unity camp, the 'palace' group fell into sharp decline. It declared that changes in Poland were a mere Soviet-approved ploy that in no way alleviated the country's plight. In 1957, the Independent Social Movement unsuccessfully pressed for the creation of local units supportive of the government, and also denied the importance of political parties, thus incurring strong opposition from Zaleski. In 1958, the Council of the Republic began another term. It had 55 representatives from four political groups: the Christian Democratic Party, Union of Polish Socialists, Convent for Struggle for Independence and the National Revival Movement. Adam Pragier was elected chairman of the Council, and Antoni Pająk became Prime Minister. With both men in the Union of Polish Socialists, popular support dwindled. To remedy this, the Council made legalism an icon.[19] Political support for the 'palace' was scant in Europe, but still held in the United States.

The PNDC was in the doldrums, too. With deep political differences between Mikołajczyk and Karol Popiel, by 1956 it had lost its status of a multiparty political body. Like the 'palace', Mikołajczyk and his supporters saw developments in Poland as a game between Władysław Gomułka and the Kremlin. Any minimalist concepts were viewed in terms of national betrayal. A maximalist programme was consistently upheld, with an emphasis on the complete withdrawal of Soviet forces from Poland, full freedom of speech and political activity, dismissal of the communist government, and free, internationally supervised elections. The unity camp was accused of defeatism.

The Provisional Council of National Unity (PCNU) contemplated holding an election. For one thing, it had been 15 or 20 years since political mandates had been won; for another, the passage of time had naturally reduced émigré élites. Although the electoral procedure had been proposed by PCNU committees in 1956, political bargaining delayed the event until June–July 1962. About thirteen thousand voters took part out of an estimated sixty to eighty thousand of those eligible; 536 elected representatives convened for the First General Congress of Poles in Britain in London in October, and chose members of the Council of National Unity. The Congress insisted that Poland must regain independence on its territories between the Oder-Neisse and the Riga Treaty line, and for an end to Poland's dependence on Moscow. In émigré affairs, it stressed the need to expand the National Treasury.[20] The Council of National Unity first met in December 1962. A new Council of Three was elected: Generals Anders and Komorowski, and Ambassador Raczyński. The new Executive of National Unity was headed by Adam Ciołkosz. The opposition blamed the Council of National Unity for refusing to renegotiate the Unity Act. In the early 1960's, opposition groups attempted to consolidate. In March 1963, the inaugural meeting of the Federation of Democratic Movements (FDM) was held in London. It was joined by the Polish Freedom Movement, Independence and Democracy, and the Socialist, Peasant and Labour parties, and concluded that Poland could aspire to independence based on an evolution of the existing situation, especially in view of growing dissent in the communist bloc.[21]

For many years, the idea had been germinating of holding a general congress of the Polish emigration. Some, like Ciołkosz, favoured giving it the clear political focus of restoring Polish independence and democratization of life. A rival concept, put forward by the Polish Ex-Combatants' Association, advocated a community basis. Politicians understood this idea as an attempt to marginalise them. Negotiations finally resulted in the acceptance of two congresses: one political, one community-oriented. Consequently, the Executive called a Worldwide Congress of Fighting Poland in May 1966, not a particularly favourable time as it nearly coincided with celebrations in Rome of the millennium of Polish Christianity. Discussions at and after the Congress were dominated by the question of Poland's eastern frontier as defined in the Treaty of Riga. Andrzej Friszke suggests that the organisers intended to make expatriate Polish communities more realistic in their political objectives.[22]

The second half of the 1960s saw a significant evolution in the position of the Peasants' Party (PSL), which increasingly gravitated toward the unity camp. It shared critical opinions of Gomułka's government and the Catholic Church. A closer conciliation, however, did not come about until the peasant leaders had left the political scene. The PSL was then headed by Józef Rzemieniewski and Franciszek Wilk, who, despite Rzemieniewski's protests, signed the PSL's entry into the Council of National Unity in December 1969. The Council elected a new Council of Three: General Anders, Ambassador Raczyński and the PPS's Alfred Urbański.[23]

In that period, the 'palace' group had little political influence and no meaningful organizational backing either in Britain or in France, although it could claim some support in the United States. Both the government, which numbered eight ministries, and the 86-strong National Council held meetings that were mostly limited to their own group. A new situation came about only when the main antagonists died: Anders in May 1970 and Zaleski in April 1972. Soon after Anders' death, Zaleski showed some willingness to compromise. In November 1970, he dissolved the Council of the Republic, replacing it by a Council of the State under Mikołaj Dolanowski. Talks suddenly broke down in January 1971, and the 'palace' reverted to its previous position, including recognising Zaleski as President. In response, the unity camp concluded in September 1971 that 'continuity based on a fictitious state of war 26 years after it ended is legally deficient and politically imprudent.'[24] This meant a return to the *status quo ante*.

Talks resumed following Zaleski's death. His successor, Stanisław Ostrowski, wanted to bury the hatchet. In May 1972, both estranged parties jointly drafted a declaration which recognised that the chief aim of the united Polish emigration was the restoration of freedom and independence to a democratic Poland, abrogation of the Yalta agreements, including the annexation of Poland's eastern territories by Russia, securing international recognition for the Oder-Neisse border with Germany, and bringing Poland and other central European countries into a united Europe. The parties of the union camp responded to this declaration in early June. It was rejected by the SN and SP under Tadeusz Drzewicki. Favourable responses came from the PPS, the Independent Social Group and the Polish Independence League. Finally, the mission to form a new government was entrusted to the Council of Three member, Urbański.[25] In July, the Council of Three dissolved both the Council of National Unity and the Executive, recognized Ostrowski as President of Poland, and dissolved itself. Ostrowski appointed General Stanisław

Kopański Inspector-General of the Armed Forces, and named a Provisional Transitory Commission, which was to serve as a temporary representative organ. Ostrowski pledged to remain in office no longer than seven years and named Ambassador Raczyński as his successor. In August, the National Treasury was integrated under a new Chief Committee.[26] No sooner had the split in legalist circles been reconciled, however, than a new split arose. Representatives of the Labour and National parties met in London in December 1972 and created a new authority, the Polish National Union, embracing Christian and national ideology. Its Council named an Executive Committee. At chairman Antoni Dargas's suggestion, chiefs of administrative branches were nominated, as had once been the practice in the Executive.[27]

As a result of the reconciliation, the building at 43 Eaton Place once again became the hub of the emigration's political activity. But problems arose when the National Council was being formed. In 1965, the Council of National Unity had decided that Poles who had obtained citizenship in countries where they had settled could also be its members. In 1973, it was agreed that those eligible to elect and be elected were all who had been Polish citizens on 1 September 1939, as well as their children, if at least one parent met the above requirement. This was an attempt to attract to the legalist circle as many communities and organizations as possible. The new National Council first assembled on 15 December 1973.[28]

The parties that remained outside the legalist circle gradually lost significance throughout the 1970s. The Polish National Union dwindled to merely the National Party and some Labour splinters. Nor did the FDM display much activity. It attacked the legalist principle, but welcomed the Polish National Union for introducing a measure of order to the Polish political scene. This, however, was undermined by factional struggles in the socialist movement. While some socialists made up the mainstay of the FDM, a segment with Ciołkosz stayed out. The PSL was in deep crisis. Chairman Wilk, having enlisted the support of London structures, cared little for other centres. A break-up followed in May 1975, when two separate party congresses met. One, held in London, re-elected Wilk chairman of the PSL. The other met in Brussels, supported by the SN, Independence and Democracy, Popiel's and Drzewicki's Labour, and a socialist faction. Both the FDM and the Polish National Union hoped to win over the PSL. With Stanisław Bańczyk elected chairman, this faction of the PSL moved into an anti-legalist position.[29]

After the mid-1970s, the emigration became acutely aware of developments in Poland. In October 1976, a Civic Relief Committee for Victims of the June Events, with Ambassador Raczyński as its head, was created in London. The Committee united many leaders of the legalist camp. This and other actions launched in support of the Workers' Defence Committee in Poland invigorated émigré communities. Hopes were raised by US President Jimmy Carter's human rights' policies. Such impulses led to renewed contact with the *Kultura* periodical in Paris and the Polish section of Radio Free Europe. Only the Polish National Union, or, in reality, the National Party, remained outside this flurry of activity.[30] When, in January 1978, Poland's Workers' Defence Committee transformed itself into the KOR Social Self-Defence Committee, the London-based Civic Relief Committee dissolved itself. Planned in its place was a Committee of Solidarity with the Democratic Movement. It was to be independent of any structures or organizations, while being at the same time an appropriately serious body. Hence, a preliminary membership list included activists from legalist circles, the FDM, *Kultura*, as well as distinguished Polish academics who arrived in the West following the anti-Semitic campaign in Poland in March 1968. The project finally fell through, however, because Ciołkosz refused to abandon the legalist cause, and without him it was impossible to win over Ambassador Raczyński and other leaders of the 'old' emigration. Consequently, aid to Poland was decentralized.[31]

In London, the extent of that aid suffered because of internal conflicts. The appointment of Kazimierz Sabbat as Prime Minister was understood by some of the former 'palace' group as signifying that the government was now in the hands of a 'mutineer'. In a speech before the National Council in October 1976, Sabbat rejected proposals to create a body in which the opposition would sit beside the government. In his turn, former Prime Minister Urbański tried to undermine the trust of legalist activists in different parts of the world in the Commission of National Treasury. Efforts to this effect were joined by Wilk's PSL. Tensions continued until elections in November 1977. Despite calls for a boycott, more than 11,000 turned out. As a result, a second General Congress of Poles in Britain met in February 1978, giving an opportunity for some members of the National Council to be elected.[32]

On 8 April 1979, Ambassador Raczyński was officially installed as President, rousing considerable emotions. The ceremony was boycotted by the PSL and 'palace' parties: the Christian Democrats, Union of Polish Socialists and Independent Social Movement. The new President was a figure of great importance. He was known in Poland and his stature facilitated contacts with 'Polish' London, which until then had been perceived as somewhat exotic. On the other hand, some émigré circles, including *Kultura*, though welcoming him, suggested departing from the existing legalism because it had become anachronistic. In their opinion, government nomenclature should be abandoned and a presidential council created instead. Such proposals were disregarded. Finally, in February 1980, Raczyński named Sabbat his successor, which disturbed former supporters of Zaleski, especially in the United States.[33]

The London-based government showed interest not only in Polish life, but also in the situation of Polish émigré groups world-wide. In the 1960s, some of these communities had been proposing the idea of a worldwide congress of expatriate Poles, the Polonia. Sceptical of the idea, Sabbat quoted an unwritten agreement of 1966 to keep the political separate from the social. A conference of the Polonia of the Free World did not come about until November 1975, in Washington, DC, with the Polish-American Congress chairman, Alojzy Mazewski, taking the lead. When, three years later, a second such event was to be held in Toronto, London legalists again raised objections, not least because the organisers had not invited the government. The warnings were not heeded and the First Worldwide Congress, 'Polonia 78 – Polonia of Tomorrow', convened in May 1978. It stopped short of establishing a Polonia organization, limiting itself to creating a Coordinating Council of the Free World Polonia. The legalist camp saw this move as a threat. It was feared that the Council could take the initiative in defining the emigration's aims. By its very existence, the Council was also a denial of any rift between the Polonia and the wartime emigration. In any case, the rift was gradually overcome in practically all countries of settlement. One exception was Britain, still inhabited by large numbers of non-naturalized Poles. The legalist camp responded to the Congress by holding a worldwide convention of political emigration: the Worldwide Congress of Solidarity with Fighting Poland met in London in September 1979.[34]

The events of the mid-1970s demonstrated that the government's preoccupations were Polish opposition and Polonia. In spite of legalistic formulations, however, the government was not a principal body, but rather one of the players. As Friszke puts it, 'Constitutional legalism was not an ultimate value for the Polonia, much less for Poland. Groups and communities that had abandoned legalism over the past decades were still in existence and could be useful partners for the Polonia as well as for domestic opposition.'[35] While Britain remained a stronghold of the legalist camp, only minor groups in other countries lent it their support.

The labour unrest that began in Poland in October 1980 and the consequent rise of the Solidarity trade union created a totally new situation, also for the emigration. The imposition of martial law led to a number of large-scale demonstrations in Britain and the creation of many relief organisations, such as the Polish Solidarity Campaign, or British Solidarity with Poland. All the while, the legalist camp maintained a fairly steady political influence and sustained unchanged divisions within it. Yet such contradictions did not impede unanimous support for Solidarity's struggle. The only exception to this unified front was the National Party, which claimed that opposition élites descended mostly from communist dignitary families allied with liberals.[36]

Kazimierz Sabbat became President on 8 April 1986, and in May appointed the government of Professor Edward Szczepanik. Political pronouncements of the time foresaw no rapid or far-reaching changes in Poland in the near future. In September 1988, a government conference was held at Fawley Court, with delegates from 13 countries. The actions of 'menders' of the communist system were criticised. The round table negotiations from February to April 1989 also divided Polish London. Sceptics, including Sabbat, predominated in the legalist camp. Developments in Poland were obscured locally by elections to the National Council in April that year. At its inaugural session in June, however, Sabbat spoke favourably of the 'contract elections' held meanwhile in Poland.[37]

During the political transformation in Poland after 1989, Poland's Prime Minister, Tadeusz Mazowiecki, paid an official visit to London in late February 1990. While he did not meet émigré authorities, he did talk by telephone with President Ryszard Kaczorowski, who had assumed office following Sabbat's death on 19 July 1989, and paid a private visit to former President Raczyński. A few days later, however, the government minister, Aleksander Hall, officially met in Toronto the Coordinating Council of the Polonia of the Free World, the chairman of the London-based National Council, Zygmunt Szadkowski, and the Minister for Domestic Affairs, Ryszard Zakrzewski. Later, at a National Council session in London, Prime Minister Szczepanik said: 'in the face of changes occurring in the country and in all of Europe, the day is drawing near when the office of the President can be passed to a successor elected by the nation.'[38]

Meanwhile, momentous changes were underway in Poland. The 'contract' Diet and freely elected Senate shortened the term of the incumbent President, General Wojciech Jaruzelski, and introduced a constitutional clause providing for a general presidential election. From mid-May 1990, official contacts between Warsaw and the government-in-exile became more frequent. The most consequential of these was a visit to London of the Senate Marshal (Speaker), Professor Andrzej Stelmachowski. On 5 November, accompanied by Ambassador Tadeusz de Virion, he paid an official visit to President Kaczorowski. Prime Minister Szczepanik, members of his cabinet and representatives of the National Council also attended. The talks focused, in the words of Stelmachowski, on 'the conclusion of the government-in-exile's mission'. Kaczorowski spoke of 'conditions of transferring the office of the President'.[39] Finally, on 22 December 1990, in Warsaw's Royal Castle, as the last President of the government-in-exile, he handed over to President Lech Wałęsa the presidential insignia: the flag of the Republic, presidential seals (one each for ink, wax and dry embossing), and the original of the Constitution of April 1935. By then, as decreed by Kaczorowski on December 20, the last government of Poland in exile, as well as the National Treasury, had been dissolved. A Liquidation Committee was appointed 'to conclude any business of the government-in-exile's institutions'. After a free election in Poland, on 8 December 1991, the National Council met for the last time.

The Liquidation Committee closed the affairs of nine ministries, 20 delegate offices, the Civil Chancery of the Republic and chapters of orders. Documents of the institutions being closed were presented to the Archive of the Polish Institute and Sikorski Museum in London. Historical items were transferred to the Royal Castle in Warsaw and the Polish Embassy in London. The National Treasury deposits (over £500,000 in total) were to be used to finance the Polonia Aid Foundation Trust (PAFT). A lesser part (£25,000) supported the budget of the Federation of Poles in Great Britain. PAFT received the lease of the 'palace' – the building at 43 Eaton

Place, London. The Liquidation Committee concluded its proceedings on 18 March 1992, and dissolved itself. This put a formal end to the existence of the Polish government-in-exile.
Translated from Polish by Tadeusz Stanek

NOTES

1. Its first term was from 23 January 1940 to 3 September 1941, and the second from 3 February 1942 to 21 March 1945. On the work of the government and Council, see E. Duraczyński, *Rząd Polski na uchodźstwie 1939–1945. Organizacja. Personalia. Polityka*, (Warsaw: 1993), *passim*; Z. Błazyński (ed.), *Władze RP na obczyżnie podczas II wojny światowej* (London: 1994), *passim*; E. Duraczyński, R. Turkowski (eds), *O Polsce na uchodźstwie. Rada Narodowa Rzeczypospolitej Polskiej 1939–1945* (Warsaw: 1997), *passim.*
2. W. Rojek, 'Schyłek misji ambasadora Kajetana Dzierżykraj-Morawskiego we Francji: grudzień 1944–lipiec 1945', *Teki Historyczne*, XX, 1993, p. 391; T. Wolsza, 'Rząd RP na uchodźstwie 1945–1949', in A. Szkuta (ed.), *Kierownictwo obozu niepodległościowego na obczyźnie 1945–1990* (henceforth KON) (London: 1996), pp. 1–2.
3. T. Towpik-Szejnowska, 'Polski Korpus Przysposobienia i Rozmieszczenia w Wielkiej Brytanii', *Zeszyty Naukowe Uniwersytetu Jagiellońskiego*, DLXIII, 'Prace Historyczne', 66, 1980, pp. 123–37; J. Morawicz, 'Demobilizacja Polskich Sił Zbrojnych na Zachodzie', in L. Kliszewicz (ed.), *Mobilizacja uchodźstwa do walki politycznej 1945–1990* (henceforth MUWP) (London: 1995), pp. 8–24; W. Leitgeber, 'Polski Korpus Przysposobienia i Rozmieszczenia w świetle dokumentów brytyjskich', in MUWP, pp. 36–62.
4. T. Wolsza, *Rząd RP na obczyżnie wobec wydarzeń w kraju 1945–1950* (Warsaw: 1998), pp. 23–30; R. Turkowski, 'Parlamentaryzm polski na uchodźstwie 1945–1972' (Warsaw: 2001), pp. 42–3.
5. R. Buczek, *Stanisław Mikołajczyk* (Toronto: 1996), vol. II, pp. 133–44; Wolsza, *Rząd*, pp. 30–36.
6. A. Friszke, *Życie polityczne emigracji* (Warsaw: 1999), pp. 103–4.
7. Ibid., pp. 107–9.
8. P. Ziętara, 'Rozłam w kierownictwie politycznym emigracji 1950–1972', in KON, pp. 39–40; A. Urban, 'Kryzys prezydencki – kryzys legalizmu 1954–1972', ibid., pp. 86–8.
9. T. Wolsza, 'Próba pojednania emigracji w 1950 r. Misja prof. Henryka Paszkiewicza', *Dzieje Najnowsze*, XXVIII, 1995, no. 4, pp. 131–4.
10. Urban, 'Kryzys', pp. 89–96; Zietara, 'Rozłam', pp. 41–3; Turkowski, 'Parlamentaryzm', pp. 130–37; for the text of the Unity Act, see W. Hładkiewicz, *Polska elita polityczna w Londynie 1945–1972* (Zielona Góra: n.d.), pp. 273–5, reprinted in A. Suchcitz, L. Maik, W. Rojek (eds), *Wybór dokumentów do dziejów polskiego uchodźstwa niepodległościowego 1939–1991* (henceforth WD) (London: 1997), document no. 53, pp. 289–93.
11. R. Habielski, 'Kryzysy prezydenckie 1947 i 1954 roku. Ich antecedencje i następstwa', in A. Friszke (ed.), *Warszawą nad Tamizą. Z dziejów polskiej emigracji politycznej po drugiej wojnie światowej* (henceforth WNT) (Warsaw: 1994), pp. 35–6; Friszke, *Życie*, pp. 190–95.

12. Ziętara, *'Rozłam'*, p. 48; Habielski, 'Kryzysy', p. 38.
13. *Polityka*, no. 21, 25 May, 1991.
14. Friszke, *Życie*, pp. 208–9.
15. Ziętara, *'Rozłam'*, pp. 49–50; A. Friszke, 'Rozłam w PPS (1956–1960)', in WNT, p. 118; Friszke, *Życie*, pp. 21–213; WD, document no. 75, pp. 355–6.
16. A. Paczkowski, 'Druga emigracja Stanisława Mikołajczyka (1954–1966)', in WNT, p. 111; Friszke, *Życie*, p. 216.
17. Buczek, *Stanisław Mikołajczyk*, pp. 236–9.
18. Friszke, *Życie*, p. 262.
19. The legal-formal picture of the situation at the time was presented by J. Gawęda, *Legalizm polski w świetle prawa publicznego* (London: 1959), *passim*.
20. Turkowski, 'Parlamentaryzm', pp. 182–9; Ziętara, *'Rozłam'*, pp. 58–9, who states that about fourteen thousand voted.
21. Friszke, *Życie*, pp. 325–6; Ziętara, *'Rozłam'*, p. 60.
22. K. Habryk, 'Polska emigracja polityczna. Historia Rady Jedności Narodowej' (Warsaw: 1972), vol. 2, pp. 206–12.
23. R. Turkowski, 'Rada Narodowa RP po zjednoczeniu emigracji 1972–1989', in KON, pp. 189–91; Friszke, *Życie*, pp. 359–62.
24. Friszke, *Życie*, p. 371; Ziętara, *'Rozłam'*, pp. 67–8.
25. T. Radzik, *Z dziejów społeczności polskiej w Wielkiej Brytanii po drugiej wojnie światowej (1945–1990)* (Lublin: 1991), p. 36.
26. Turkowski, 'Rada', pp. 202–4; K. Trzeciak, 'Zarys historii Skarbu Narodowego', in KON, pp. 371–2.
27. Friszke, *Życie*, pp. 378–9.
28. Turkowski, 'Rada', pp. 206–8; Friszke, *Życie*, p. 382.
29. S. Wąsik, 'Federacja Ruchów Demokratycznych', in KON, pp. 556–62.
30. Friszke, *Życie*, pp. 402–6.
31. Ibid., pp. 407–8.
32. Ibid., pp. 412–3.
33. Ibid., pp. 416–8.
34. R. Habielski, 'Emigracja' (Warsaw: 1995), p. 32.
35. Friszke, *Życie*, p. 433.
36. G. Hart, 'Polish Solidarity Campaign', in T. Piessakowski (ed.), *Akcja niepodległościowa na terenie międzynarodowym 1945–1990* (London: 1999), pp. 450–78; A. J. Bohdanowicz, 'British 'Solidarity with Poland' Campaign', ibid., pp. 485–90.
37. Friszke, *Życie*, pp. 473–4.
38. 'Przekazanie insygniów prezydenckich do Kraju', in Z. Błażyński and R. Zakrzewski (eds), *Zakończenie działalności władz RP na uchodźstwie 1990* (London: 1995), p. 37.
39. Ibid., p. 41.

5

The Poles in Scotland, 1940–50

Peter D. Stachura

The periodic emigration and settlement overseas of some ten million Poles since the Partitions of the late eighteenth century have been fundamental to Poland's development as a state and nation, and provide the general historical context within which any single episode may be viewed. The main pressures behind this movement were, at different times, economic, social, political, ideological and military in nature, and usually a mixture of these. The expansionist ambitions and repressive policies of Poland's neighbours, and frequently occupiers, also played a decisive role. A distinction has to be made, of course, between voluntary and enforced emigration. An example of the former was the seasonal migration of Poles from the beginning of the nineteenth century to large estates and industrial centres in Germany, and subsequently to the factories and coal mines of northern France and Belgium. In the second half of the century, the United States became the principal destination of Polish emigrants.[1]

On the other hand, involuntary emigration accompanied this trend at particular junctures. The failed November Rising (1830–31) and January Rising (1863–64) against the Russians triggered fresh waves of unwilling Polish exiles, mostly to France, while the Second World War inaugurated the most tragic and entirely involuntary chapter in the history of Polish emigration. The ultimate consequence of all these large-scale movements has been the formation of substantial émigré Polish communities, especially in the United States, Canada, Brazil, Argentina, France, Germany and Britain. This chapter considers a small but distinctive segment of this phenomenon, namely, the Poles who began arriving, entirely as involuntary immigrants, in Scotland in 1940 and those who remained there in the early years after the end of the war.[2]

The remnants of the defeated Polish armed forces succeeded in escaping through Hungary and Romania to continue the fight alongside their French and British allies. Many of them fought in the French campaign in 1940, but were forced to escape again with the fall of France in June of that year. From that date, not only the exiled Polish government under General Władysław Sikorski (1881–1943), but also thousands of Polish troops found a haven in Britain with the aim of continuing the fight. While Sikorski's government was based in London, the Polish troops, soon numbering about 20,000, together with 3,000 civilian refugees, were sent for largely logistical reasons to hastily constructed camps in Scotland. With Germany threatening to invade the south-east of England, where British troops were attempting to regroup following the disaster of Dunkirk, the War Office decided that Scotland was the most appropriate place for the Poles. Above all, they could begin to reorganise in sparsely populated, but accessible regions relatively undisturbed. Before long, the sight of columns of Polish troops marching through the streets of towns and cities drew enthusiastic applause from Scottish onlookers.[3]

In these early days, the Poles were well received by the Scots, who regarded these strangers from a distant and unknown country, speaking an incomprehensible language, with a combination of intense curiosity and admiration. This favourable view was reinforced by the Poles' invariably smart appearance, impeccable manners, strong sense of discipline and overall exemplary behaviour. Only a handful of them, for instance, were ever prosecuted for violating the Allied Forces Act (1940).[4] The impressive contribution of Polish fighter pilots under RAF command to the Battle of Britain in autumn 1940 also helped relations with their hosts.[5] Local authorities and welfare organisations gladly arranged accommodation, canteens, receptions and free travel on public transport for the Poles, who were at first organised in tented camps near the small Lanarkshire towns of Crawford, Biggar and Douglas, and later in Cupar, Forfar and other towns. Public money was raised, such as the Polish Forces Comforts Fund in Glasgow and Edinburgh,[6] and Poles were often invited by Scots into their homes. The Lord Provost of Glasgow, Patrick J. Dollan (1881–1963), was so supportive that he was nicknamed 'Dollański' by the grateful Poles.[7] The holding of gala days, concerts, exhibitions featuring the work of Polish artists serving in the forces, the exchange of gifts, commemorative plaques, standards and other mementos became a regular feature of everyday relations between the Poles and Scots, whose open friendliness the Poles deeply appreciated.[8] As one Polish soldier recalled:

> When we arrived in Scotland, a country which none of us had really any knowledge of, we did not know what to expect. At first, it was a strange and uncomfortable feeling to be so far from our beloved and tragic homeland, but within a short time we were made to feel very welcome at every level and almost part of the Scottish community, which certainly eased our plight. We were in the fight against German tyranny together. And we were especially popular with the girls, who came to our dances in large numbers![9]

Another wrote, in somewhat more poetic vein: 'We smiled at this serene country. From the first day we felt surrounded by a warm and exciting atmosphere of cordiality. We saw a country more civilised than many of the Continental states, bright, picturesque, and extremely attractive.'[10] In fact, it was not at all surprising, in view of this happy relationship, that during the war several thousand marriages took place between Polish soldiers and local Scotswomen who, as a result, had to forfeit their British citizenship and accept the status of aliens.[11]

The Poles reciprocated Scottish hospitality by lending a hand to local activities, such as harvesting, by taking up defensive duties along the east coast in anticipation of a German invasion, and by training for the greater military tasks ahead. A visit in March 1941 to their headquarters at Moncrieff House, just outside Perth, by King George VI (1895–1952) and Queen Elizabeth (1900–2002) further boosted the morale and prestige of the Polish troops. The vitality of their presence was underlined by the number of schools established with British government assistance for Polish children, most of whom were orphans: Dunalastair House, Pitlochry, was a notable example.[12] These schools were supervised jointly by the Polish Board of Education in London, attached to the Polish government, and the Scottish Education Department, whose inspectors frequently compiled favourable reports about them, praising their standard of teaching and the attainment level of pupils.[13] For adults, a series of educational facilities were created, including the Polish Medical School at the University of Edinburgh, the Polish Agricultural

School, the Polish Centre of Electro-Technical Training and the Polish Commercial College.[14] In 1945, they had a combined enrolment of 1,358 students.[15]

Consolidating all these endeavours from both sides were a number of prominent public figures and organisations, including several noted aristocrats and academics, such as Sir Hector Hetherington (1888–1965), the Vice-Chancellor of the University of Glasgow, and the Catholic Church hierarchy. Some of them helped promote a new organisation established in April 1941, the Scottish–Polish Society.[16] With branches quickly set up in many towns, especially where the Poles were stationed, the Society succeeded under the energetic leadership of John J. Campbell, a Glasgow solicitor, in fostering further links between both communities by organising language and history classes, concerts, dances, seminars, conferences, medical aid and other activities. Poles and Scots joined in roughly equal numbers, and as the war dragged on and the politics of the Allied alliance became more complicated, the Society emerged as a vociferous advocate of the recreation of an independent and sovereign Poland.[17]

This halcyon period of mutual support and respect began to fade before finally crumbling, however, as a direct consequence of the inclusion of the Soviet Union, Poland's erstwhile enemy, in the Allied Grand Alliance against Germany in 1942.The whole military and diplomatic course of the war was now changed in a way that was fundamentally detrimental to the Poles. The Soviet Union's contribution on the Eastern Front was increasingly admired in Scotland and the rest of Britain, helped by a government-inspired, skilfully coordinated pro-Soviet propaganda campaign, whose equally important aim was to put the Poles and their government in as unflattering a light as possible, by depicting them as politcally unrealistic and something of a nuisance to the Allied enterprise. Even worse, the Poles were soon to be branded as anti-Semites and fascists as well,[18] notably by a number of Labour MPs, including Tom Driberg (1905–1976), who was himself of Jewish background and was later uncovered as a Soviet agent[19] Even when Stalin (1879–1953) broke off diplomatic relations with Sikorski's government in 1943 over the Katyń Massacre and was known to be already organising a communist regime to take over Poland at the end of the war, his image and popularity remained undisturbed.

The Red Army's inexorable advance on the Eastern Front ensured that the tide of popular and official opinion in Scotland and Britain as a whole turned decisively against the Poles. The Polish interest, as defined and represented by General Sikorski's government, became expendable, and this was poignantly accentuated by the decision of the Tehran Conference in December 1943 to allow Stalin a more or less free hand over Poland's future eastern border. By that time, the Poles had also suffered the loss of their leader in July 1943, although their political cause was certainly already doomed. Thus, the impressive military contribution that the Poles made to the final victory over Nazi Germany was not sufficient to reverse this official and popular pro-Soviet outlook. From the Polish troops in Scotland had been formed, most notably, the First Independent Polish Parachute Brigade (September 1941), and the First Polish Armoured Division (February 1942), which, led by General Stanisław Maczek (1892–1994), had distinguished itself in the campaigns in Normandy (Battle of the Falaise Gap), Belgium, Holland and northern Germany in 1944–45.[20] In 1945, the Poles, steadfast allies from the first until the last day of the war, and victors, were none the less forced to pay a catastrophic and undeserved territorial and political price at the Yalta Conference. The awful reality in Poland was that one totalitarian tyranny had simply been replaced by another, only this time with British and American approval, if not connivance.

If the Poles in Britain as a whole were devastated by the political outcome of the war, their situation in Scotland also further deteriorated, particularly once it became clear that a large majority of them – some 36,000 in 1946,[21] – were unwilling to return to a communist-dominated Poland. After all, that outcome was the antithesis of what they had fought for. In Scotland, powerfully entrenched left-wing groups in the trade unions and Labour Party, who feared for the impact of the Polish presence on housing, jobs and food supplies, and pro-Soviet sympathies in the country at large, resulted in the anti-communist and anti-Soviet Poles being attacked as 'warmongers', 'landlords', 'anti-Semites' and 'fascists'. A Labour MP stated bluntly in the Commons that the Poles were 'greatly resented' and unwelcome in Scotland.[22] Their Catholicism compounded the problem, in central Scotland at least, where traditional sectarianism reappeared amid the post-war austerity. The first anti-Polish rally was organised by the militant Protestant Action Society in Edinburgh in June 1946.[23] A number of violent incidents were recorded in various parts of the country; Poles were liable to be insulted in the street and by neighbours, and also faced petty discrimination in the workplace, schools and over housing.[24] They were quickly made to feel unwanted interlopers.

The Poles were also made to feel unwelcome by the newly elected Labour government of Clement Attlee (1883–1967), which wanted them all to return to Poland as soon as possible. The Treasury, with an eye on the huge financial cost of the war, was most reluctant to subsidise the Poles any longer, especially as they numbered about 250,000 in Britain by 1946. Only when the British government finally realised that the large majority of the Poles would not willingly return to a communist Poland, did it begin to accept that they would have to be allowed to settle in this country.[25] The Polish Resettlement Corps (1946–49) was accordingly set up to find civilian jobs for the demobilised Polish troops.[26] Notwithstanding the award of a government gratuity to help them on their way, it was in these unforeseen and unpropitious circumstances that the Poles became involuntary immigrants in a country that they believed had sold them out politically when it had mattered.

Between 1945 and 1950, the number of Polish-born persons in Scotland declined markedly as many of them sought employment in England or even emigrated overseas, leaving just 10,603, of whom 90 per cent were male and under 40 years of age.[27] Although recognisable Polish communities emerged in several towns and cities, noticeably in Glasgow, Edinburgh, Dundee, Falkirk and Kirkcaldy, the Poles soon scattered across the country. In 1950–51, there were 1,200 Polish-born persons in Edinburgh (895 of whom were male), 1,164 in Glasgow (975 males), 332 in Kirkcaldy, 309 in Dundee and 660 in Stirlingshire (608 males).[28] Many originated from the areas of eastern Poland now annexed by the Soviet Union, so that they literally no longer had a home to which they could return.[29] In any case, almost all took their sojourn in Scotland to be temporary.

In the meantime, the Poles had to find jobs to sustain themselves and, where applicable, their families. Despite the role of the Polish Resettlement Corps, this task was often frustrated by the hostility towards them of certain important trade unions, including the Amalgamated Union of Engineering Workers and National Union of Mineworkers, as well as by the Scottish Trades Union Congress.[30] But as the demand for labour grew in the harsh winter of 1946–47, the situation eased somewhat, to the benefit of all concerned.[31] Even so, many Poles had to accept heavy, unskilled, manual and poorly paid work in coal mines, steelworks and other manufacturing industries.[32]

For those Poles from a professional background and those who had been career officers in the armed forces, the adjustment to civilian life in a generally inhospitable climate was even more stressful, for their qualifications were usually not recognised. Consequently, they were compelled to retrain as watchmakers, bookkeepers and similar, which meant that they lost the social and economic status and prestige they had enjoyed in Poland before the war. Even General Maczek, one of the most outstanding and highly decorated Allied commanders of the war, was forced to find menial employment. The most obvious exception to this depressing pattern were medical doctors, some of whom had graduated from the Polish Medical School, which had been established in the University of Edinburgh from 1941 until 1949.[33] A few others had been able to graduate in law and veterinary science from the universities in Edinburgh, Glasgow and St Andrews.[34] At the same time, a small number of unqualified Poles, usually younger and from a peasant or working-class background, felt they now had nothing to lose and everything to gain in these new circumstances, especially if they were able to become self-employed in a trade or small business. One or two went on to make money, although sometimes by breaking ranks with their fellow Poles and cooperating with the communist regime in Warsaw and its consular representatives in Scotland. Because a relatively large number of former army officers and professionals followed General Maczek in settling in Edinburgh, the Polish community there had much more of a middle-class character than, for example, its counterpart in Glasgow, Kirkcaldy or Falkirk.

Temporary residents or not, and partly in response to the hostility they were experiencing, the Poles resolved to ameliorate their situation by creating their own organisations and social centres whose essential purpose was to preserve a sense of 'Polishness' while resisting integration and assimilation into Scottish society. This move seemed all the more important as their wartime educational establishments were being rapidly wound up by the British authorities.[35] The largest and most important new organisation was the Polish Ex-Combatants' Association (SPK), which from 1946 had branches in major towns. It nurtured Polish patriotic and cultural traditions.

The profound significance to Poles of their religion led to the establishment in 1948 of the Polish Catholic Mission in Scotland, and Polish priests were soon on hand.[36] Saturday-morning Polish language classes for children were also organised, although with mixed results, particularly if, as happened quite often, the teacher moved on after a relatively short period to another part of the country in search of employment and/or more suitable accommodation. The Scottish–Polish Society continued to support the Polish community and tried to counter anti-Polish feeling through meetings, newspaper articles and contacts with sympathetic Conservative MPs, but its membership and influence had declined considerably by the end of the decade.[37] The Poles themselves tried from time to time to lessen the antipathy towards them by issuing direct appeals to the Scots. For instance, in Edinburgh, in 1946, they called for their understanding and vowed 'not to stay one day abroad after the real liberation of Poland'.[38]

Although the Poles were not homogeneous in social, occupational or educational terms, and were prone to querulous factionalism, they were bound closely together by their devotion to Catholicism and their emphatic rejection of the Soviet-imposed communist regime in Poland. They looked forward to the collapse of this regime and its replacement before long by a truly free and independent government. In relation to Scottish domestic politics, such attitudes resulted in their rejection of the Labour Party and the trade unions as socialist and pro-Soviet, a view dating from the stance taken by many on the political left in Britain to the Polish–Soviet War in 1919–20.[39] Accordingly, and in stark contrast to their Catholic co-religionists in Scotland, the Poles looked to the Conservatives for support.

The early post-war era witnessed, therefore, the wary emergence of an embryonic, but fairly substantial, Polish community in Scotland that was characterised by feelings of insecurity, anxiety, resentment and anger. Scotland was so different from the Poland they had left behind – the language, social conventions, culture, religion, even the food and weather! They were the most reluctant of immigrants, yet felt they had no choice but to remain until the situation in Poland had changed for the better. If they had arrived in 1940 as a result of military exigencies, their stay after 1945 was motivated by political and ideological factors, thus underlining the link with the main pattern of Polish emigration and settlement until the Rising of 1863–64. By 1950, however, their hopes of returning to Poland were already fast disappearing as the Cold War developed. There would be no triumphant military crusade to liberate Poland from Soviet subjugation and communism. Instead, enforced and permanent exile in a somewhat unfriendly and insular Scotland beckoned. Once again, strenuous demands would be made on the Poles' traditional resilience and unquenchable spirit as a new and uncertain chapter in the long history of the Polish *Emigracja* began.

NOTES

This is an abbreviated version of my paper to the international conference, 'European Immigrants in Britain, 1933–1950', held at the German Historical Institute, London, on 7 and 8 December 2000.

1. P. S. Wandycz, *The Lands of Partitioned Poland, 1795–1918* (Seattle: University of Washington Press, 1984), pp. 193–238, 275–88.

2. For general background, K. Sword, with N. Davies and J. Ciechanowski, *The Formation of the Polish Community in Great Britain, 1939–50* (London: School of Slavonic and East European Studies, University of London, 1989); K. Sword, *Identity in Flux. The Polish Community in Britain* (London: School of Slavonic and East European Studies, University of London, 1996); J. Zubrzycki, *Polish Immigrants in Great Britain. A Study of Adjustment* (The Hague: Martinus Nijhoff, 1956), and *idem, Soldiers and Peasants. The Sociology of Polish Migration* (London: Orbis Books, 1988); T. Kernberg, *The Polish Community in Scotland* (Ph.D. thesis, University of Glasgow, 1990); A. Carswell, *For Your Freedom and Ours. Poland, Scotland and the Second World War* (Edinburgh: Scottish United Services Museum, 1993); P. D. Stachura, 'The Polish Minority in Scotland: 1945 until the Present', in *idem, Poland in the Twentieth Century* (London: Macmillan, 1999), pp. 113–34.

3. Archive of the Centre for Research in Polish History, University of Stirling (ACRPH), A. MacLean File, memorandum of July 2000.

4. National Archives of Scotland (NAS), Scottish Office Home and Health Department, HH057/00990 provides details of individual cases, 1941–43.

5. A. Zamoyski, *The Forgotten Few. The Polish Air Force in the Second World War* (London: John Murray, 1995), for a full account.

6. *Glasgow Herald*, 11 July 1940, p. 10; 24 July 1940, p. 3; 19 September 1940, p. 2.

7. Ibid., 31 January 1963, p. 6, for his obituary. Dollan held office from 1938 until 1941, when he was knighted.

8. Many of these gifts were included in the exhibition organised at the Scottish United Services Museum, Edinburgh Castle, in 1993–97, and in the towns where Polish troops were stationed there are numerous signs of their presence. There is also the cemetery for Polish soldiers in Perth, and other specific plots are located in cemeteries in various towns. Many plaques and memorials were introduced in the post-war years, particularly in those towns that had enjoyed a close association with Polish troops, for example, Duns, Kirkcaldy, Glasgow, Leven (home of the Polish Parachute Brigade), St Andrews and, as recently as May 2002, Biggar. More wartime examples are cited in the *Glasgow Herald*, 28 October 1940, p. 7, and 10 April 1941, p. 8; and in the *Stirling Journal and Advertiser*, 6 March 1941, p. 5.

9. ACRPH, A2: personal statement by Mr A. Marchlewski (pseudonym), June 2000. A brief narrative of life in Scotland at that time is provided in the memoirs of Mr Jan A. Dorosz, a member of the Polish 10th Mounted Rifles Regiment, in

the Archive of the Polish Institute and Sikorski Museum (APISM), Ref. KOL 158. See also D. M. Henderson (ed.), *The Lion and the Eagle. Polish Second World War Veterans in Scotland* (Dunfermline: Cualann Press, 2001).

10. *Glasgow Herald*, 20 August 1940, p. 6. Two years later, the friendliness was still strong: see ibid., 7 July 1942, p. 4.
11. Sword *et al.*, *Formation*, pp. 401, 404.
12. NAS, Scottish Office Education Department, ED26/370, letter from Dr T. Sulimirski to Secretary of the Scottish Education Department, 7 July 1941; see also ACRPH, the *Dymitr File*, concerning a one-time headmaster of Dunalastair School.
13. NAS, ED26/370, HM Inspector's report on Dunalastair School, 12 May 1943, when 51 pupils were enrolled, and letter from Dr T. Sulimirski to Scottish Education Department, 6 July 1943.
14. Ibid., ED26/374 and 375, various memoranda for 1945; ED26/376, HM Inspector's report, 3 September 1945.
15. Ibid., ED26/370, report of June 1945. For more extensive documentation, see APISM, Ref. A.19: Ministry of Religious Affairs and Education, 1941–45.
16. ACRPH, the *Thornton Private Papers*, records of the Scottish–Polish Society, membership lists for 1941–44; and the *Glasgow Herald*, 3 July 1941, p. 3.
17. Ibid., the *Thornton Private Papers*, correspondence files for 1943, including letters to John J. Campbell. For a broader survey of the Society, see L. Koczy, *The Scottish–Polish Society. Activities in the Second World War. An Historical Review* (Edinburgh: privately published, 1980).
18. C. Andrews and V. Mitrokhin, *The Mitrokhin Archive. The KGB in Europe and the West* (London: Penguin Books, 2000), p. 158, for details of Soviet agents in positions of responsibility in the British government and media conducting this propaganda; M. Kitchen, *British Policy Towards the Soviet Union during the Second World War* (London: Croom Helm, 1986), pp. 100–03; A. Polonsky (ed.), *The Great Powers and the Polish Question, 1941–1945* (London: Orbis Books, 1976), pp. 170–71, letter from Eden to Churchill, 24 December 1943.
19. *Glasgow Herald*, 6 April 1944, p. 6; 7 April 1944, p. 6; 29 April 1944, p. 4. For Polish refutations, see ibid., 12 April 1944, p. 4, and 4 May 1944, p. 5. For more on Driberg, see Andrew and Mitrokhin, *Mitrokhin Archive*, pp. 522–6; D. Engel, *Facing a Holocaust. The Polish government-in-exile and the Jews, 1943–1945* (Chapel Hill: University of North Carolina Press, 1993), pp. 127–37.
20. See A. Suchcitz, *Poland's Contribution to the Allied Victory in the Second World War* (London: Polish Ex-Combatants' Association in Great Britain, 1995), pp. 3–16; T. Modelski, *The Polish Contribution to the Ultimate Allied Victory in the Second World War* (Worthing: privately published, 1986).
21. *House of Commons Debates* (*HCD*), Fifth Series, vol. 427, col. 790, figures as of 15 October 1946.
22. Ibid., vol. 423, col. 2233, statement of 6 June 1946.
23. Stachura, *Poland in the Twentieth Century*, p. 118.
24. *HCD*, Fifth Series, vol. 431, col. 53, reference of 3 December 1946; Sword, *Identity in Flux*, pp. 48, 156, 162–7.
25. *HCD*, Fifth Series, vol. 419, cols 1363–4, government statement of 21 February 1946.
26. Ibid., vol. 420, cols 1876–78, statement of 20 March 1946.
27. NAS, GRO006/00289, Census of Scotland 1951, vol. III, general vol., (Edinburgh: HMSO, 1954), table 36, pp. 55–6.
28. Ibid., vol. I, part 1, City of Edinburgh, table 30, p. 30; part 2, City of Glasgow,

table 16, p. 32; part 4, City of Dundee, table 16, p. 34; part 17, County of Fife, table 16, p. 36; Part 31, County of Stirling, table 16, p. 31.

29. T. Ziarski-Kernberg, 'The Polish Community in Scotland since 1945', in P. D. Stachura (ed.), *Themes of Modern Polish History* (Glasgow: Polish Social and Educational Society, 1992), p. 67.
30. *Glasgow Herald*, 21 September 1946, p. 2.
31. *HCD*, Fifth Series, vol. 433, cols 197–8, ministerial statement, 20 February 1947.
32. Ibid., vol. 452, cols 189–90, ministerial statement, 29 June 1948; Zubrzycki, *Polish Immigrants*, pp. 66, 81–6; E. Stadulis, 'The Resettlement of Displaced Persons in the United Kingdom', *Population Studies*, 5, 1952, part 3, pp. 210ff., 219ff.
33. Details in W. Tomaszewski (ed.), *In the Dark Days of 1941* (Edinburgh: privately published, 1992), pp. 1–7; and the *Glasgow Herald*, 24 March 1941, p. 7.
34. APISM, Ref. A.19, Ministry of Religious Affairs and Education, miscellaneous memoranda 1941–45.
35. NAS, ED26/376, HM Inspector's recommendation in report, 17 October 1947, and ED 26/375, letter of 5 April 1948 from the Principal of the Polish Vocational College to the Scottish Education Department.
36. ACRPH, the *Thornton Private Papers*, memorandum of 14 February 1949 from the Catholic Council of Polish Welfare. See J. Gula, *The Roman Catholic Church in the History of the Polish Exiled Community in Great Britain, 1939–1950* (London: School of Slavonic and East European Studies, University of London, 1993).
37. ACRPH, the *Thornton Private Papers*, correspondence file for 1946–47, with many letters to and from John J. Campbell. See also membership lists for 1948–49.
38. Ibid., the *Thornton Private Papers*, appeal entitled, 'To Our Scottish Hosts', circulated by the Council of Polish Societies in Edinburgh, August 1946.
39. ACRPH, A2, personal testimonies of former Polish Army personnel; and ibid., the *Thornton Private Papers*, correspondence file for 1946–47.

6

General Stanisław Maczek and Post-war Britain

Evan McGilvray

Following the overrunning of most of Europe by Germany during 1939 and 1940, Polish soldiers sought refuge in the United Kingdom (UK) until such time as they would be in a position to return to the fray. At first, the British people and press were sympathetic to the Poles as 'our gallant and tragic allies'. However, the first episodes of women in London spitting at Poles in uniform were recorded in 1944.[1] What had changed the situation so dramatically was the entry of the Soviet Union into the war on the side of the Allies, following the German invasion in June 1941. Polish criticism of Soviet behaviour in eastern Poland 1939–41 had either gone unnoticed or unchecked. After 1941, with the Soviet Union on the Allied side, criticism by the Poles was no longer welcome. The Western Allies simply failed to understand Polish misgivings.

The Labour Government that was elected in Britain in July 1945 seemed to promise a brighter future. It was expected to provide better prospects for servicemen returning from the war, in contrast with the First World War, when a 'land fit for heroes' turned out to signify unemployment, slums and the means test. However, the new administration had a strong socialist content and showed rather a lot of pro-Soviet sympathy, which was also marked in the trade union movement and was translated as being anti-Polish.

The most obvious setback for the Poles during 1945 was the occupation of Poland by the Red Army as it swept towards Germany. In July 1945, the British government transferred recognition of the exiled Polish government in London to the Soviet-sponsored provisional government in Warsaw, thus stabbing its wartime ally in the back while recognising a stooge of the Soviet Union. A crumb

of comfort was offered in the form of a statement that the British
government would not force back to Poland any of the 250,000 Poles
who had served under British command. This was to prove a difficult
policy to pursue, because the anti-Polish campaigns being organised
by the British press, especially the socialist *Daily Worker* and the
Reynolds News, had raised hostility among the working class towards
Poles. Even during wartime, these two publications had referred to
the Poles as 'fascist reactionaries', 'landlords' and 'Jew baiters', terms
of abuse normally reserved for the enemy, while ignoring Polish
military achievements.[2]

After the war, the anti-Polish campaign took on a new form by
playing on the traditional and deep-rooted fear of foreign labour felt
by the British working class. Poles were not only depicted as fascists
and reactionaries living in luxury at the British taxpayers' expense.
They were also portrayed as threatening the British labour market
with their alleged huge numbers, and in turn ruining the maintenance
of full employment, bringing down the British standard of living
and wages, destroying the hard-won liberties of the trade unions,
accelerating the housing shortage and eating food that the British
could hardly spare. With the trade unions riddled with communists,[3]
there were lots of 'useful idiots', as Lenin once remarked of Western
socialists, who could strive to wreck plans and produce an anti-Polish
backlash that would detract from the Soviet Union's misdeeds in east
and central Europe as it consolidated its new empire. There were
still those in the House of Commons, however, who endeavoured to
protect the Poles from reactionary socialists. Members of Parliament
continued to ask the government if it would still honour its pledge
that not a single Pole who had served in the West would be forcibly
repatriated.[4] But when the question of granting British citizenship to
members of the Polish Armed Forces arose, the Prime Minister,
Clement Attlee, was already beginning to fudge the issue,[5] which
resulted from the xenophobia of the British working class, which had
just elected and supported the Labour government. And, of course,
the problem remained of what was now to be done with the Poles,
most of whom had refused to return home.

Another concern was what was to be done with the Polish Army
in Italy, the so-called 'Anders' Army', which, by the beginning of
1946, was beginning to pose an international problem. Once again,
the press in northern industrial centres ran a story that these Polish
troops were reactionary and fascist, and some Yorkshire newspapers,

quoting *Pravda* as their source,[6] reported that they were planning for war in Italy. It was well known that these men would not consider returning to Soviet-occupied Poland, as most of them had been victims of the Soviet occupation in 1939–41. There was a need, therefore, to discredit the Anders' Army before it arrived in the UK, which served only to add to the anti-Soviet sentiment already evident among Poles in Britain. It finally transpired, however, that the *Pravda* story was based upon hearsay and rumour and soon fizzled out.[7]

The Polish provisional government had quite a problem with General Władysław Anders, as he was one of the most outspoken critics of the Soviet Union and its policies towards Poland, and demanded the disbanding of the Polish units under British command. The Polish government applied extra pressure by decreeing that all their (Polish) armed forces abroad were disbanded and had to return to Poland. Anders was very quick to point out that Poland was still not free.[8] Ernest Bevin, the British Foreign Secretary, retorted that the Polish government was being less than helpful.[9] This was followed by tit-for-tat incidents, which indicated the tension in Anglo–Polish relations. Warsaw emphasized that if the British dismissed Anders and other high-ranking Polish officers, the situation could be eased.[10] This was an obvious case of blackmail, but why the British had to concede so rapidly is not obvious. The only explanation would seem to be the need to keep the working class, especially the trade unions, on side, and not appear to be too anti-Soviet. Bevin stressed the need for Britain's friendship with Russia.[11]

The British government, especially Bevin, did all it could to persuade Polish servicemen to return to Poland within the confines of the British pledge that no Pole would be returned to Poland against his will. Bevin urged that the Poles should do so without delay, claiming that it was their duty to return to Poland.[12] Indeed, in 1947 he finally admitted in the Commons that if he had had his way all of the Poles would have been *sent* back to Poland.[13] He was well known to be anti-Soviet, but also had a history of anti-Polish activities. Bevin was famous for his involvement in the blacking of the loading of the ship *Jolly George* in the London docks during the Polish–Soviet War of 1919–20, and in the successful trade union-led campaign, 'Hands off Russia', which denied Poland much-needed shipments of armaments during that war.[14] He was certainly anti-Catholic and, by implication, anti-Polish.[15] The British, instead of being grateful for the Polish contribution to the Allied war victory, wanted the Poles banished, and retreated into xenophobia as accusations began to fly regarding housing and food. The irrationality of the British position, especially in the organised labour movement, was shown once the government finally revealed that the country was facing a labour shortage, especially in labour-intensive industries such as mining, building, agriculture and most certainly textiles.[16]

Anders and other senior Polish commanders understood that the British could not continue to preserve Polish personnel as an armed force under British command, and agreed to cooperate in their disbandment. It was decided that there would not be some form of overnight discharge of the Poles, but instead an orderly demobilisation, as with British servicemen.[17] Before the end of March 1946, the disbanding of the Anders' Army was announced. At a stroke, a bone of contention between Warsaw and London was removed. It was revealed that, in response to a questionnaire sent to these Polish troops in autumn 1945, one third had agreed to return to Poland. Bevin at once urged all of the Poles to return home, pointing out that the Polish government had promised that nobody who had served with the British would come to any harm unless they had served in the German Armed Forces or were guilty of high treason or common crimes.[18] This did not give any form of guarantee to men from eastern Poland who now found that their homes were in the Soviet Union and who were, therefore, technically Soviet citizens. The Soviets did not issue any form of guarantee to the Poles.

The tension between the Warsaw regime and the British government, even though slightly abated by the disbanding of the Anders' Army, still continued and resulted in Warsaw expressing strongly its dissatisfaction with the lack of speed with which the British were demobilising the Polish servicemen.[19] The reaction was swift. At a special meeting on 17 May 1946 of the Joint Consultative Committee (JCC), a junior committee from the Ministry of Labour and the Trades Union Congress (TUC), the various options concerning the disbanding of the Polish Armed Forces and the problems of the labour shortage were outlined. It was argued that demobilised Polish servicemen would be able to fill vacancies in British industries, especially textiles and mining. The general council of the TUC agreed to the formation of what became known as the Polish Resettlement Corps (PRC), but the TUC wanted certain conditions met in order to guarantee its further support and assistance – above all, that the Poles were to be employed only as a last resort, wherever

British workers were either unwilling or unavailable to be employed. The Poles were to be discharged and placed in the PRC, with the aim of transferring them to civilian life as soon as possible. Polish servicemen who already had approved jobs were to be discharged immediately. The PRC was designed to be short-lived, and as soon as resettlement was complete, it was to be wound up. The Ministry of Labour oversaw the PRC, while the TUC and the Employers' Congress agreed to cooperate.[20]

British cooperation with the PRC failed to materialise, however, especially where trade unions at a local level were concerned. Much of the focus of anti-Polish feeling was not published in national newspapers, but was concentrated in the regional newspapers in areas where large numbers of industrial workers lived and worked, and where the trade unions had influence. For example, under the lurid headline, 'Storm breaks over Poles at TUC', the Bradford-based newspaper, *Telegraph and Argus,* reported the 78th Annual Trade Union Congress, held between 21 and 25 October 1946. Apart from mentioning a vote that failed to admit Poles to the labour movement, most of the report abused Poles, who were referred to, once again, as 'fascists' and 'Jew-baiters'. In addition, they were accused of 'strutting around Liverpool' as if they owned it. A further report seems barely credible as a Scots trade union leader from Irvine claimed that Polish troops used bayonets in an attempt to break up a trade union meeting. This prompted British troops to collect machine guns from their barracks. Only the timely arrival of the local police apparently prevented a massacre.[21] Such reporting to a targeted readership was cynical, and designed to aggravate further a group of people who were already fearful for their own job security and future by presenting them with an enemy who was allegedly becoming all too visible in post-war Britain.

Not all Labourites, however, were against the Poles. Michael Foot, the future Labour Party leader, wrote in the *Daily Herald,* which was not noted for its sympathy for the exiled Poles, that they had been the first to fight the Nazis. Foot wrote at a time when the Warsaw government had condemned the Poles as traitors (to Poland).[22] In the Labour Party journal, *Tribune,* an article compared the treatment of the 16 arrested Polish resistance leaders and their transfer from Poland to Moscow with that of the infamous Moscow trials of 1931–36.[23] Clearly, some members of the Labour Party were able to see beyond the Soviet lies, even if rank-and-file trade union officials could not. There were also other sources of sympathy and criticism within parliament concerning the government's treatment of exiled Poles and their homeland. One MP quoted from an American publication that stated: 'Poland, our ally, had been treated worse than our enemy, Germany. Germany is to be administered by the four great powers. Poland is to be administered by Soviet Russia.'[24] In November 1945, a complaint was made in the Commons that there was a 'deadly silence' concerning Polish servicemen becoming British or Empire citizens.[25] Despite this sympathy, it was soon confirmed in parliament that the Poles were to be treated as foreign workers.[26]

How did the Poles fit into this poisonous atmosphere in post-war Britain? One case study, that of General Stanisław Maczek, indicates that they did not. He had fought the Germans from 1939 until 1945. In particular, under his command, the First Polish Armoured Division had fought a brilliant campaign in north-west Europe from the time of its arrival on the Continent in August 1944. The Division had been instrumental in the Allied breakout from the Normandy peninsular as well as responsible for the liberation of large parts of Belgium and Holland, including the Dutch city of Breda, in autumn 1944. Before 1939, Maczek had fought for the Polish Army during the wars of liberation, including the Polish–Soviet War of 1919–20. Earlier, as a Habsburg subject in partitioned Poland, he had been conscripted in 1914 into the Imperial Austrian Army, in which he served with distinction until autumn 1918, when the Austrian Empire fell and he was able to return to the newly independent Poland. During the September campaign of 1939, Maczek was the only Polish commander to retrieve territory from the Germans.

Maczek retired from the army on 9 September 1948. Unlike most other distinguished Polish officers, he avoided politics. He had conducted his career in a manner more usual in a Western army: that of loyalty to the state and not to personalities. However, Maczek was now faced with the loss of status and a secure income, both of which he had enjoyed as a professional officer in inter-war Poland. The British failed to give him any form of position in a staff college or anywhere else. For them, he was just another exiled Polish officer. Even though Maczek spoke good English,[27] he was nearly sixty years of age and also had a family to provide for. To make the situation even more difficult, his youngest daughter, Magdalena, was handicapped and needed constant care. A further impediment to integration for

Maczek and many other Poles was that they believed they would be able to return to Poland within a decade, as the Soviet occupation was thought likely to be temporary. As a result, they were more concerned with the interests of the Polish community than with that around them. This naturally prevented assimilation, assuming that the British wanted to mix with the Poles.

The British failure to offer Maczek any form of suitable work was not only a disgrace, but also very short-sighted. He was an experienced and able commander, and had also been an inter-war intelligence officer, involved in work against the Soviet Union, and no doubt had developed an insight into the Soviet mind. However, such credentials may not have suited government policy of the late 1940s. Once again, the British had missed a great opportunity. Instead of being feted in the United Kingdom, as he was after the war in Holland,[28] Maczek become a bit of a non-person at the very time when he lost his Polish citizenship, because of his defiance of the communist government in Poland.

Typically, Maczek did not complain about his circumstances. His military career had thrown up so many difficulties that his new life as a civilian in exile in an unfriendly and ungrateful country did not bother him too much. The British did not provide him with a pension and, of course, he did not receive any form of gratuity from the Polish authorities, who regarded Maczek and his fellow officers as traitors and renegades. To provide for his family he took various jobs, all relatively menial, given his intelligence, experience and former professional status. At one time he was a barman in a hotel owned by one of his former soldiers, and also worked in a sports club and a shop.[29] The Dutch government, however, did award him a pension, in gratitude for his actions in Holland during the war.

Maczek decided to settle in Edinburgh. This made sense, as Scotland was where the First Polish Armoured Division had been formed in 1942 and where a great number of Poles chose to settle. By moving there, Maczek was able to stay out of exile politics, which were found in most Polish communities. Their fratricidal arguments and squabbles did little to enhance the Poles' reputation and eventually split them. Instead, Maczek, aided by his wife, Zofia, continued to serve his former division by providing humanitarian assistance, especially to those who had been invalided as a result of their war service. He steadfastly refused to allow them or anybody else to raise funds for himself or his family.[30] But he made it possible for his son, Andrzej, to graduate from Oxford with a degree in chemistry and later to gain a doctorate in his chosen field.

In 1961, Maczek's autobiography was published. It was essentially a military account, in which he steadfastly refused to criticise his treatment in Britain by the authorities. In fact, he made no comment about post-war Britain and life in exile. The distribution of the book, however, provides a comment on the genteel poverty that he and his family had to endure. Maczek, in his travels to visit certain officers, left a number of copies of his book with them to sell on his behalf. In this way, he was able to realise a fuller value from it instead of having to pay a percentage to a bookshop or bookseller[31] – assuming that a stockist could be found, as the book was published in Polish. In the mid-1960s, it was translated into French but not into English.[32]

General Maczek became the unofficial leader of the Polish community in Scotland.[33] By keeping aloof from the foolish quarrels of exile, he was able to retain his dignity, which drew people to him. Throughout his exile, he continued his loyalty to the inter-war Polish Republic and never recognised the Polish Peoples' Republic, despite overtures made to him during the 1980s. He continued to work with his 'boys', who were becoming pensioners themselves. His persona was also used as a tool against the communist regime in Poland. On his 80th birthday, in 1972, reports of the celebrations and the speeches commemorating the occasion were broadcast on Radio Free Europe.[34] Maczek was presented as a source of an alternative Poland and something quite different to communist propaganda. His history was a counterbalance to the official Soviet version of the Second World War, which ignored, for instance, the Soviet invasion of Poland and the Katyń Massacre. He was even evidence of the Polish victory in the Polish–Soviet War of 1919–20.

Even the British remembered Maczek on his 80th birthday, when it was announced that he was to be the guest of honour of the Commander of the Army in Scotland during the Edinburgh Tattoo, to be held later that year. The ever-grateful Dutch also celebrated his birthday, which included a concert from Holland, broadcast both on BBC2 and Radio Free Europe.[35] The modest Maczek told *The Scotsman* that he preferred to be called Mister rather than General, and that he did not like being 80![36]

Maczek's 95th birthday, in 1987, revealed changes in Poland, as the first official notices of the occasion were made. He received celebratory telegrams from Generals Kamiński and Skibiński, who had served in the First Polish Armoured Division before returning to post-war Poland and continuing their military careers with the communist Polish Peoples' Army.[37] Even more interesting was a report in the communist youth magazine, *Sztandar Młodych*, which referred to Maczek as the 'last hussar of the Republic' (*'ostantni husarz Rzeczypospolitej'*).[38] There were also reports of his birthday in the Polish press, including the popular *Ilustrowany Kurier Polski*[39] Clearly, the Polish authorities were feeling the need to turn to such eminent exiled figures in some perverse hope of propping up their rapidly collapsing regime.

The General's century was a cause of great celebration. Once again, cards and notices poured in from all over the world. By this time, Poland had shed communism and was once again a free and independent country. Sadly, Maczek was too frail to return there, while his native Lwów still lay in the newly independent Ukraine. The tributes on his birthdays are testament to his enduring legacy in the free world. The British may have forgotten him until he was 80, but the Belgians and especially the Dutch, including young people born after the war, wrote to Maczek, expressing their gratitude for their freedom that he and his men had delivered.[40]

General Maczek died on 11 December 1994, at the great age of 102. The Poles, Scots and Dutch mourned his passing. After a funeral in Edinburgh, he was buried in Breda, the scene of one of his greatest victories and alongside his dead comrades. His legacy will be primarily that of his military achievements. His life after retirement was spent virtually in obscurity, but was difficult, owing to changes in British foreign and domestic policies that adversely affected the exiled Poles. Maczek was never allowed to retrieve his professional and social status, although he continued to receive the devotion of his former soldiers as much as he continued to serve them and retain his loyalty to the pre-war Polish Republic.

NOTES

1. J. Zubrzycki, *Polish Immigrants in Britain: A Study of Adjustment* (The Hague: Martinus Nijhoff, 1956), pp. 80–81.
2. Ibid., p. 81.
3. A. Bullock, *Ernest Bevin, Foreign Secretary: 1945–1951* (London: Heinemann, 1983), p. 220.

4. *Hansard Parliamentary Debates*, Fifth Series, vol. 415, 29 October–16 November 1945 (London, 1945) col. 389, 30 October 1945.
5. *Hansard*, vol. 414, cols 23–5, 9 October 1945.
6. *Telegraph and Argus* (Bradford), 4 February 1946.
7. Ibid.
8. *Yorkshire Post*, 18 February 1946.
9. *Yorkshire Post*, 19 February 1946.
10. *Yorkshire Post*, 21 February 1946.
11. 'Task of Growing Together is Purpose of my Policy: Mr. Bevin', *Yorkshire Post*, 22 February 1946.
12. *Yorkshire Post*, 21 March 1946.
13. *Hansard*, vol. 437, cols 1740–41, 20 March 1947.
14. N. Davies, *Orzeł Biały Czerwona Gwiazda: Wojna polsko-bolszewicka 1919–1920* (Kraków: Wydawnictwo Znak, 1998), pp. 178–80.
15. H. Young, *This Blessed Plot: Britain and Europe from Churchill to Blair* (London: Macmillan, 1998), p. 50.
16. *Yorkshire Post*, 10 January 1946; *Telegraph and Argus*, 18 January 1946.
17. *Weekly Hansard*, no. 9, 15 March–21 March 1946, cols 1879–89.
18. *Yorkshire Post*, 21 March 1946.
19. 'New Polish Demand – Demobilisation of Armed Forces', *Yorkshire Post*, 7 May 1946.
20. *Yorkshire Post*, 23 May 1946.
21. *Telegraph and Argus*, 25 October 1946.
22. *Hansard*, vol. 413, col. 1110, 24 August 1945.
23. *Hansard*, vol. 413, col. 1112, 24 August 1945.
24. *Hansard*, vol. 413, col. 1113, 24 August 1945.
25. *Hansard*, vol. 416, col. 801, 23 November 1945; *Tribune*, 11 May 1945.
26. *Hansard*, vol. 416, cols 1510–11, 29 November 1945.
27. The author is grateful to Antoni and Paulette Polozyński of Pudsey, West Yorkshire, for their personal memories of General Maczek.
28. See Renata Maczek's schoolgirl account of her family's tour of Holland in the late 1940s in Archive of the Polish Institute and Sikorski Museum, London, (APISM), Kol. 298/53.
29. P. D. Stachura, *Poland in the Twentieth Century*, (London: Macmillan, 1999), p. 91; *Glasgow Herald*, December 1991, in APISM, Kol. 298/44.
30. Stachura, ibid., p. 91.
31. Antoni Polozyński in conversation with the author, November 2001.
32. S. Maczek, *Avec Mes Blindes: Pologne, France, Belgique, Allemande* (Paris: Tomar Publishing, 1967).
33. Stachura, *Poland*, p. 91.
34. APISM, Kol. 298/31.
35. Ibid.
36. *The Scotsman*, 1 April 1972.
37 APISM, Kol. 298/35.
38. *Sztandar Młodych*, 1 April 1987, in APISM, Kol. 298/37.
39. *Ilustrowany Kurier Polski*, 31 March 1987, in APISM, Kol. 298/36.
40. APISM, Kol. 298/42. See P. D. Stachura (ed.), *Themes of Modern Polish History. Proceedings of a Symposium on 28 March 1992 in Honour of the Centenary of General Stanisław Maczek* (Glasgow: Polish Social and Educational Society, 1992).

7

Homeland Memories and the Polish Community in Leicester

Kathy Burrell

All theories of nationalism recognise that there is a strong link between national identity and the national homeland.[1] The mother/fatherland can be perceived to be the natural land of the forefathers, a tangible link with the nation's ancestors, joining together current citizens with those who came before into one large family directly rooted in common soil. National boundaries are also arguably the most influential system of regulating power divisions in the world, allowing certain spaces to be internally regulated in a national manner, through national institutions. It is not surprising, therefore, that territorial attachments form a key component of exiled national identity for migrants who find themselves outside their homelands. For the Polish diaspora in particular, memories of the homeland are highly significant in the maintenance of a Polish identity outside Poland. Experiences of war, forced migration and exile have fundamentally changed the personal relationship with the Polish homeland, while at the same time a strong awareness persists of the tragic nature of Poland's recent history, which has heightened the importance of territorial independence for the completion of the national project. In addition to this, 50 years of living outside Poland has further complicated the issue of homeland loyalty, almost forcing the creation of new Polish spaces. This chapter, therefore, will explore the changing relationship of the Polish 'community' in Britain with the Polish homeland itself, concentrating on the small but well-established Polish group in Leicester, a population that peaked in 1961 with the enumeration of 1,509 Polish-born people in the city.[2]

The research itself was based predominantly on 28 oral history/in-depth interviews that used a 'life-history' methodology, allowing the respondents to talk freely about their personal experiences, emotions and perceptions.[3]

The horrific experiences of Poland in the Second World War have been well documented, and while the domestic population spent the war under occupation, the German and Soviet invasions of Poland resulted directly in widespread population movements that would not otherwise have taken place.[4] Those who had joined the Polish Army, of course, had to spend much of the war outside Poland fighting with the Allies, clinging to the hope of an eventual return to a free homeland. The majority of the Polish people who ended up in Britain at the end of the war, however, had left Poland in different circumstances, enduring forced removal from their homes on the eastern side of Poland and deportation to Siberia at the hands of the Soviet Army. Indeed, it is estimated that as many as 75 per cent of all Poles who came to Britain after the Second World War had experienced this type of deportation.[5] The shock and disruption brought about by these invasions therefore cannot be over-emphasised. For all the Poles interviewed in Leicester, the war is still perceived to be the pivotal changing point in their lives, whatever their personal narrative, and memories of migration are inextricably bound up with images of the early years of occupation.[6] One man shared the following account of his deportation to Siberia by Russian forces in 1940:

> Then, in 1940, when the Russians occupied our area, we slept in our house, and in the middle of the night, about one o'clock in the night time, the Russians came to our house and started banging with the guns on the door. We had to get up quick and they told us what to do. We had one hour to take everything we could, because we were going to different places in Russia. We didn't know where they were going to take us. In one hour, we packed everything we could, then they put us on the sledges to the railway station. That night and that winter was very cold, about 28 degrees below zero, it was very, very cold. They brought us to the station and they put

us in the wagons. There were about 38 people there, it was very crowded. We travelled to Siberia for about two weeks.[7]

Arrival in Siberia brought no relief from the fear and uncertainty of the journey, as the following man's memories demonstrate:

After we arrived in Siberia, we were just thrown out of the train onto the snow and were told by the Russians, 'here you live and here you die', which to me meant nothing. But I realised what they meant because there was no food, no shelter, people were freezing to death, and from one third from the transport, about a third died off. And the Russians sent everybody to the working camps.[8]

In 1941, an amnesty was reached with the Russian government, allowing the release of the Polish deportees in the Soviet Union. This resulted in the formation of the Second Polish Corps under General Anders, and the large-scale movement of the survivors unable to join the forces to civilian camps throughout India, Africa and the Middle East. These journeys to the safety of the camps brought further suffering, however, and as Keith Sword comments, this second movement resulted in more deaths than had occurred because of the previous deportations.[9] One woman, who had survived deportation, described her family's journey out of Siberia:

In 1941, we had an amnesty. General Anders. We managed to come out of Siberia, the four of us, my mother, my two brothers and myself; somehow we survived, perhaps we came from good healthy stock. From Siberia to Caucasus, it took three months. We were travelling three months in the cattle trucks. It was full of lice, full of lice, in Siberia there were so many bedbugs ... When we arrived, my brother joined the Polish Army. It was severe winter, very, very severe winter. We had typhoid there ... At the beginning of August, the Polish Army came and took us. I remember this, this is how we left Russia. On the 6th of August, we crossed the border; we went to Karachi, to Mombassa, then we landed in the jungle in Uganda.[10]

While these experiences dominated the interviews, only around 75 per cent of the people spoken to had lived on the eastern side of Poland and survived deportation. Of the testimonies collected, for example, one woman had been sent to a German labour camp, another had fled to Czechoslovakia, and three of the first-generation men had originated from western and central Poland and had joined the Polish forces at the outbreak of war. What all these different routes out of Poland have in common, however, is the subsequent shared experience of dislocation from the national territory. Regardless of the passage taken, the respondents in Leicester were united in their perceptions of themselves as exiles, after a return to the homeland was effectively ruled out at the end of the war by the Soviet-directed communist takeover. One woman tried to put into words this feeling of being exiled:

> At that time, we really believed, as it was the wartime, the forties, that soon after the war we really did think we'd go back. The war will be over and we will go back to Poland. We were extremely disappointed when it wasn't so. I don't think many people would have chosen to stay away at that time.[11]

Another man recalled the frustration felt towards the Allies for 'betraying' Poland to the Soviets at the Yalta Conference:

> There was a bit of hard feeling, there still is, by the older generation, that we were sold out by Churchill and Truman to Russia. Even though we fought in the war they just handed us over on a plate to the Russians, and for what? A lot of soldiers just shot themselves, committed suicide, there was a terrible hard feeling.[12]

One former member of the Polish Air Force also commented on the widely held fear that going back to Soviet-dominated Poland would be dangerous:

> Some went back to Poland. But, as you know, when the war finished, Churchill, Roosevelt and Stalin signed an agreement at Yalta, and part of Poland has become under Russian occupation, and there was a Polish communist government. Only a few went. Of those who had been in the Air Force who had fought for Britain, about one hundred people went back, and they were exterminated in Poland when they went there, they were just murdered or went to prison. All knowledge of them disappeared, even today we don't really know what happened to them. Many officers were murdered by the secret police.[13]

Furthermore, the shifting of Polish borders to the west at the end
of the war conceded vast tracts of land in the east (later to become
the Ukraine and Belarus) to Russian control, leaving all those who
had been sent to Siberia literally with no homes to return to. As one
man explained:

> All of us, with the exception of one or two per cent, were from
> eastern Poland, which is now in Russia, the southern part is
> Ukraine, the upper part in Belarus. We couldn't go back there, so
> to go back to a Poland that we hardly knew, that wasn't an option,
> really. Nobody had a house … because nobody had that so there
> was no reason to go.[14]

The Poles, therefore, not only came to Britain and Leicester as a
result of invasion or deportation, but also had little choice but to
remain as exiles after the war.

REMEMBERING THE HOMELAND

Through the course of the interviews, it became clear that these
experiences of exile are closely related to how the Polish homeland
is remembered and depicted in Leicester. For those who had been
forced from their homes the image of Poland has been particularly
tinged with tragedy, but for everybody interviewed, personal exile
was perceived to fit in very easily with the broader history of the
Polish nation. Just as this generation had been disrupted by foreign
invasion and occupation, generations of Poles had suffered in a
similar way before them. The most striking example of this proved
to be Poland's history in the nineteenth century, when the nation
lost its territorial rights for 123 years at the hands of Russia, Prussia
and Austria.[15] During these partitions, Polish national identity had
to be sustained without a territorial base, and relied on an extensive
underground commitment to keeping the Polish language, religion
and traditions alive. As the following man's testimony illustrates,
awareness of this era, and of Poland's historic vulnerability generally,
is an important part of being Polish:

> The Germans took the west part, the Russians took the east part
> and the Austrians took the south part of Poland. Well, it was a very

difficult period for Poland. We had been invaded by Muslims, by
Tartars, Turks, and eventually Poland became so weak that other
people took advantage of our country. The Second Partition
came in 1793 and the Third in 1795. Poland stopped existing as
a country, but people got used to it, and just had to get on with
living. That lasted until Marshal Piłsudski came to power … in
1918, Poland became a country again. In 1920, the Russians tried
to invade Poland again … there was a bloody battle just outside
Warsaw and the Russians were defeated. That's how we lasted until
1939. It wasn't very long, then the Second World War came. Poland
is a country in a very difficult geographic position. The Germans
were always greedy to take part of Poland, the Russians invaded
Poland, we just couldn't cope with all that.[16]

Several interviewees also commented on the similarity between
these times and the deportations to Siberia in 1940, where any out-
ward signs of 'Polishness' had to be hidden from the Soviet troops.
Of course, exile generally, and deportation to Siberia in particular,
have a long history, as this same man recounted:

After the Third Partition, there was a lot of uprising, people tried
to free themselves, but they were defeated and many of these
people were sent to Siberia. My grandfather and his family were
sent to Siberia as well. When Poland became a country and we
started fighting for freedom, they returned from Russia.[17]

The historical need to fight for the freedom (*wolność*) and independence (*niepodległość*) of the Polish homeland has left a powerful
legacy among the Polish people interviewed in Leicester.[18] Despite
the reclamation of Polish freedom with the fall of communism in
1989, the fears about Poland's territorial security persist. Too many
memories of war and invasion, coupled with a strong historical
consciousness, have ensured that while those living in Poland can
presumably try to get on with living their lives in a new era, those
watching from abroad are still preoccupied with old anxieties. One
woman voiced some of these frustrations:

There is a fear now, the population are afraid of joining the
Common Market, the reason being it will make it easier for our
neighbours, for example for Germany. And they are doing it

already, buying land very cheaply, buying it illegally through the back way. And there is a fear that once you lose your land, you lose your independence again. So, there is a fear that joining the Common Market, they will gradually lose what they have, and lose it in another way, not in war, in a peaceful way. People know that they couldn't trust the Russians; they knew that Russians were the enemy for centuries, but they don't actually see that they can't always trust the West. When you live in the West you realise that everybody looks after number one, and I don't think that's recognised in Poland, and I think before they realise it, it may be too late.[19]

The centuries of partitions and border changes have also left more confusing ramifications for Polish national identity in exile. It has proved to be quite difficult to hold on to a 'pure' national identity, untouched by the redrawing of Polish territorial boundaries and the foreign influences of the Partitions' era. One second-generation woman highlighted this problem when she spoke about how she had been taught about Polish history and the changing borders at the Polish Saturday School:

We did Polish history and geography. It made me smile, because they had this map of present-day Poland, but what happened was Poland shifted, and what the Poles told us was, this is Poland, but this bit, with Vilnius and down there, used to be Poland but the Russians pinched it off us. So they made out not that Poland is here and it has moved, but that it used to be bigger. They didn't own up that, actually, we were given a bit from the Germans. They kept that quiet. They didn't deny it, but the way they said it, it was like this bit should really be ours.[20]

This loss of land in the east to Russia not only physically deprived people of their homes, but has caused tension within the group, calling into question the Polish credentials of some of those whose birthplaces are now in Belarus and the Ukraine. Another second-generation woman recounted how her father had been accused of being Russian rather than Polish, because he had come from the east:

It's a running joke with the Poles that everyone is from Warsaw. No one wants to admit they are from the east. I remember someone years ago in the Polish community was saying, 'oh, so your father is Russian', because I never used to get embarrassed about saying my father was from the eastern side, Belarus. And this particular man in the Polish club used to say, 'oh, so you're not Polish, you're Russian'. I know where my parents were born, and I actually found a map and I was going to take it. I thought you are being so petty because the borders kept changing. Years later, he came to me and said he went to see his relatives in Belarus, and I thought 'crikey', you used to say that I'm Russian, but you are from the same part of Poland! But people used to be really embarrassed and reluctant to say that they came from that part of Poland, maybe because they thought they would be called Russian.[21]

Despite more openness in recent years, there are still suspicions that some people who claim to be Polish may not necessarily be genuine, as the same woman who spoke about the Saturday School commented:

You've got to be careful with some Polish people, some of them, it makes you wonder whether they are half-German, or half-Ukrainian, depending on which side they are on. And you can sometimes tell by their surnames if they've been changed a bit. A lot of Ukrainians pretend to be Polish.[22]

As has been highlighted, similar ambiguities exist regarding the nationality of those from the area of northern and western Poland that had fallen under German control through partition. Another second-generation woman, for example, spoke of how her father had been called up into the German, rather than the Polish, Army during the Second World War:

My dad comes from the north of Poland, which was under the German Partition. When the war started, they were left alone, although he had a sister whose husband was called up into the German Army. That's one of the things about Poland: the boundaries are sometimes quite blurred. In the middle of the war, they were taken to do forced labour in Germany, but then he was called up into the German Army. I think that's why he never talked about it much.[23]

The interviews undertaken have also revealed the persistence of myths and even strategic omissions in the presentation of Polish history. Gdańsk, for example, is spoken about with great pride, understandably so, for its role as the birthplace of Solidarity, but nothing is mentioned about the German heritage of the city, which had only had its name changed back to Gdańsk from Danzig after the Second World War.[24] As an illustration of this, one man began his testimony with the following assertion: 'I was born near Gdańsk, where the Solidarity movement started; it's now famous. My last place of working was Gdańsk, in the shipyards.'[25] Similarly, much less is said about Poland's history as a powerful, even aggressive, country in the fifteenth and sixteenth century than about the more recent role as a tragic but valiant victim of expansionist neighbours.[26]

At times, this mythology also stretches to the personal memories of the homeland, illustrating that for those who do not return regularly, their images of Poland can be both overly romantic and outdated. This is certainly an accusation that several second-generation respondents have levelled at their parents' generation. As one woman commented: 'A lot of Poles I feel sort of froze during the war. And they have these very, very fond memories of pre-war Poland ... They live, the older generation, very, very much in the past.'[27] The language and traditions followed by the Poles in Leicester are from the pre-war era, and are now almost out of place in contemporary Poland, particularly in the big cities. Travelling to Poland and discovering that the 'Polishness' learnt in Leicester is different from the national consciousness felt in the homeland can be a disturbing experience for the second generation, as this woman admitted:

> I went [to Poland] just before Solidarity ... We had a traditional Christmas Eve supper which we always have here, but they didn't have what we had. Even though they were so poor, they had got this whole smoked salmon, which we had never had before. I remember feeling really disappointed. There's us struggling to keep up these traditions and they go and have smoked salmon and fried cod and things like that. I think we tend to fossilise traditions that people over there just wouldn't do.[28]

Even the traditions themselves can be elevated to an unrealistically romantic status, considering that not everybody in Poland would have followed them in the same way. Another woman, for example, described how her mother had only learnt some of the Christmas Eve traditions when she came to Britain, not having come across them before in Poland:

> To be honest, not many people in the cities would use all the traditions. My mum actually learnt some of the traditions when she came here. Her best friend was from a village and so she knew all these traditions, and she learnt about Christmas Eve and having twelve different courses. So she did it, but she didn't do little courses, she did big ones. These adults were eating all night. She used to spend weeks preparing.[29]

Returning to find a very different country from the one that had been left behind, and subsequently recreated in the imagination for 50 years, can therefore be a huge shock, especially for the first generation:

> The country changes. You see, in half-a-century, things change quite a lot … for the first time, when I went to the village where I was born and where I went to school, I looked at it and said to my sister, 'What have you done to the country?' I remember my part of Poland where I come from was more or less the richest part of Poland, and when I went there, oh, my God! Nothing painted, nothing repaired, they think everything is OK, and I say everything is not OK, it's not. It was better fifty years ago than it is now.[30]

Enforced exile has, consequently, dislocated the relationship with the homeland in the long term. After the war, it was almost impossible for people to return to Poland to live: now the Poland of their memories is not only a long distance away geographically, but is also lost in time.

TRANSNATIONAL CONNECTIONS

Of course, links with the homeland do not have to rely entirely on myths and memories. Despite being in exile, most of the people interviewed had managed to visit Poland before 1989, although at times this was an uneasy experience. As one man explained, it was

1. General Władysław Sikorski.

2. King George VI and Queen Elizabeth, accompanied by various military chiefs, including General Władysław Sikorski (on far right), visit the Polish 24th Lancers Regiment in Arbroath, Scotland, March 1941.

3. A group from the Polish 24th Lancers Regiment, soon to become part of the legendary First Polish Armoured Division, prepare to lay a wreath at a war memorial in Arbroath, Scotland, July 1941. The soldier holding the wreath is Władysław Stachura.

4. Members of the Polish Wartime Cabinet, 1942: (from left)
K. Popiel, J. Kwapiński, W. Sikorski, S. Kot, General M. Kukiel and
S. Mikołajczyk.

5. Second-generation Polish children in national costume during a
Corpus Christi procession, circa June 1960.

6. The new Cabinet of the Polish Government-in-Exile is sworn in at 43 Eaton Place, London, the seat of government, circa 1962. August Zaleski, President of the Republic, is second from left, and Prime Minister Antoni Pająk is third from left.

7. Generals Stanisław Maczek and Władysław Anders, 1969.

His Holiness
Pope John Paul II

Historic visit to England,
Scotland and Wales

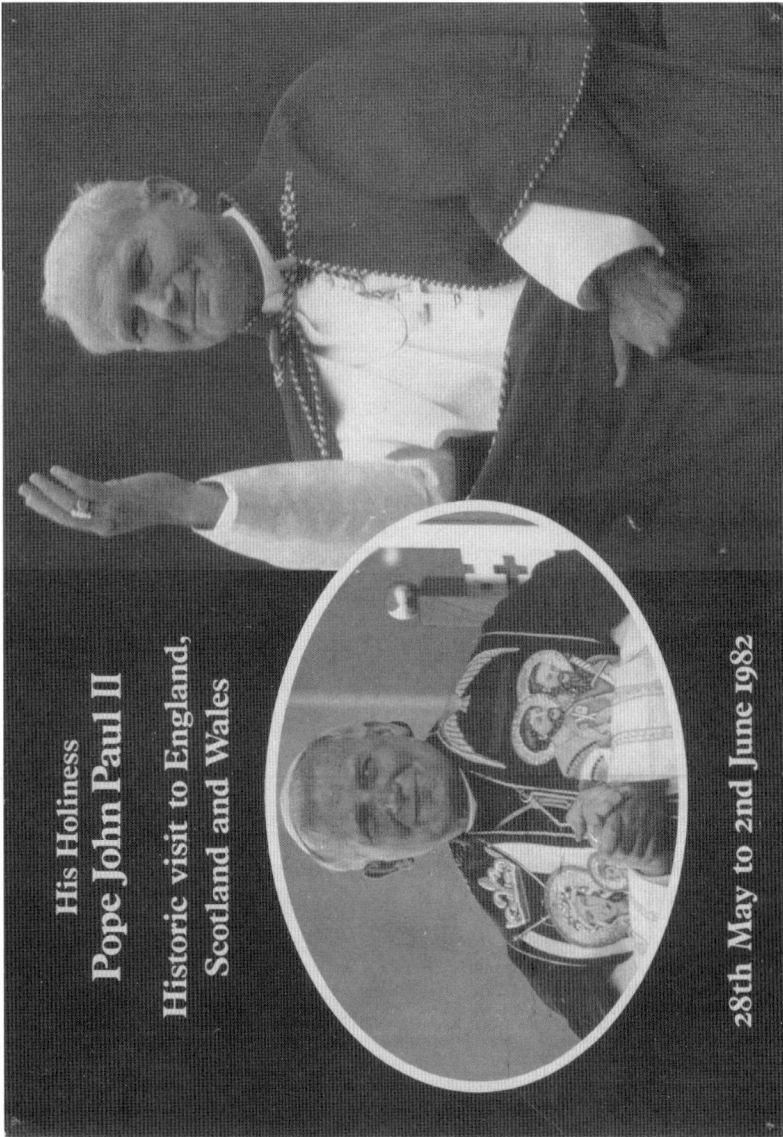

28th May to 2nd June 1982

8. Pope John Paul II's visit to Britain, 1982.

9. Ryszard Kaczorowski hands over the state insignia of the Second Republic to Lech Wałęsa, the newly elected President of Poland, the Royal Caste, Warsaw, 22 December 1990.

10. Never to be forgotten: the unveiling of a plaque commemorating the wartime presence of Polish troops in Biggar, Lanarkshire, 30 May 2002. In attendance, a colour party of the Polish Ex-Combatants' Association, the Polish Consul General in Scotland, Mr Wojciech Tyciński (second from left) and a Polish Embassy representative (far left).

even difficult to keep in close contact with friends and family: 'Well, we tried, but it wasn't wise. All letters were censored and there were no such things as telephone conversations. All telephone conversations were taped.'[31] Since the fall of communism, however, travel and communication opportunities have proliferated, enabling a new relationship to be formed with the homeland, based on a more realistic and less romantic understanding. As Benedict Anderson asserts more generally: 'the communications revolution of our time has profoundly affected the subjective experience of migration.'[32] All of the first generation, for example, have access to the satellite television station TV Polonia, either through the parish and ex-servicemen's clubs, or at home. Although it is mainly the older people who watch TV Polonia, one of the teachers at the Saturday School confirmed that the younger Poles also watch Polish programmes: 'When they come to visit their parents, they [the second generation] watch it then, and the children from Saturday School, I know they watch it because their parents watch it, and they know when I mention something, they know what I am talking about.'[33] These programmes provide a powerful reminder of the homeland, transmitting exclusively in the Polish language, and broadcasting, for example, regular concerts of traditional folk-dancing and singing. TV Polonia, however, also allows a more authentic image of Poland to be accessed, showing the changes in society and politics that the Leicester Poles have not been able to experience first-hand. While these changes have unfortunately come too late for many of the Poles in Britain, developments like these, alongside the increased travel options, have ensured that those who want to keep up to date with homeland affairs can do so.[34]

NEW POLISH SPACES

While the Polish homeland has been an important focus for the Poles in Leicester, the people interviewed demonstrated that the relationship with Poland is not exclusively outward-looking. Aspects of Polish life have also migrated to Britain with the Poles themselves. Firstly, a community began to develop with the establishment of formal institutions in the city, for example, the Saturday School in 1952, the Ex-Servicemen's Club in 1956, and eventually the acquisition of a church and adjoining buildings in 1965. Beyond the church and clubs, extensive networks of small businesses, family and friendships have also combined to create distinct Polish spaces in Leicester, as one second-generation woman recalled:

> We had this big, extended family in Leicester, and the community was like this even bigger extended family. There was a Polish shop on Narborough Road where you could buy Polish sausages and things like that. Other Polish people went there as well, so you would see them there sometimes. You would go to a Polish doctor. I think that there was the sense that you were helping somebody out by giving them business, giving them a helping hand. Most of the people you knew were Polish. Our early life was very Polish.[35]

As another woman commented, these networks ensured that generally most people within the community would know of the other Poles in the city:

> I'm not saying we know everybody, because we don't, but there is always somebody that knows somebody. There are very few people who are actually so very, very isolated … [my friend] is a teacher at the Polish school for many, many years now, so the children that were children are adults now. So, if you mention a name she says, 'oh, yes, I don't know very much about their children', but she knows the name. It's a very closely knit community from that point of view.[36]

Bringing Poland to Leicester has not always depended on these types of networks and institutions, however, and in the private sphere of the household, Polish traditions, mythical or otherwise, have been carefully sustained and passed on to the younger generations. For example, when asked about keeping up Polish customs, one first-generation woman replied, 'yes, even my children do. Although they are married to English people now, when it is Christmas Eve, we all eat the food that my mother told me how to cook, and we all enjoy it. We keep on doing it.'[37] Christmas and Easter celebrations, in particular, have been maintained with great care, as another woman described:

> Christmas must be celebrated as normal in Poland: fasting on Christmas Eve, the evening is family dinner, and the family dinner

is without any meat. First, we always share the bread, the wafer, and there was a man who had no family and we always sent one of our sons to bring him back for that family dinner, or leave a space, leave a chair for an unexpected guest. And, then, everybody has presents as normal, after dinner, and singing carols ... Easter is the same story. On the Saturday before Easter, absolutely it is a must to go to the church with food in baskets to be blessed. This is absolutely necessary ... there is food to eat and the main thing is the eggs. Some are painted in different colours, painted in really artistic patterns. I have been doing that myself, it takes time. And, of course, those baskets are always decorated, with flowers.[38]

Other traditions have also survived, such as All Souls' Day and name days, but there are also more general cultural customs that are remembered in Leicester, the most striking being that of hospitality. Several interviewees mentioned the phrase *gość w dom, Bóg w dom,* literally meaning, 'guest in the house, God in the house', claiming that even though this was an old tradition, the historical attitude of welcoming friends and strangers into the home has continued:

Gość w dom, Bóg w dom, it is very important. People invite each other more than English people ... there would be a traveller, for example, in pre-war times, and they would knock on the door, and the father of the household would ask how far he is intending to go. And if he says he has to go far, he would say, 'look, why don't you stay here for the night and go in the morning?'. It would be that sort of hospitality ... they visit each other [in Leicester] on Sundays. Families know each other, they visit each other, I know it happens. They move from one house to the other with the children. The children play and they have a chat, sit together and talk.[39]

Of course, there are limits to how successfully Polish life can be translated to life in Britain and Leicester. As one man commented, while the building of a Polish community here has been welcomed, it is not the same as living in Poland itself:

After fifty years in this country, I haven't grown into this ground. I still belong there with my mind and my soul, I belong there. Unfortunately, fifty or sixty years being outside makes a difference, but not in the basic belief that I belong there and I am a Pole. It hasn't changed at all. I still haven't got the British citizenship, I am an outsider, absolutely. As a principle, of course, I could apply and get it years ago, but I don't see any reason why I should. Mind you, I belong to the Anglo-Polish Society. I'm an active member there. I respect my friends, and feel quite comfortable and good in the presence of my English or British friends, but I'm still basically a Pole.[40]

CONCLUSION

For the Poles in Leicester, the homeland has provided a focal point to which a continued national consciousness can be anchored while in exile. All the time the Poles could not return to Poland, even for visits, efforts were made to bring Polish life to Britain, to ensure that Poland was never forgotten. As soon as it was possible, links with the homeland were resumed, and a different yet significant relationship was created. These developments, however, are typical of most migrant groups. Although people might grow apart from their national territory while they are away, the homeland continues to form an important cultural and national reference point. What makes the Polish experience of exile different is the historical symmetry between the fate of the individual and the fate of the nation. The freedom and independence of the homeland is more important for the Polish exiles in Leicester, and Britain more generally, because the memories of dislocation from Poland resonate with everything learnt and told about modern Polish history. If any myths about the geography of the homeland are sustained, or even created, in exile, this only serves to demonstrate how intimately entwined the personal narrative has become with the changing territorial boundaries of the nation.

NOTES

1. For a good introduction to the theories of nationalism, see U. Ozkirimli, *Theories of Nationalism – A Critical Introduction* (Basingstoke: Macmillan, 2000). For an in-depth discussion of territory and nationalism, see G. H. Herb and D. Kaplan (eds.), *Nested Identities – Nationalism, Territory, and Scale* (Oxford: Rowman & Littlefield, 1999).
2. Figure taken from the *1961 Census Report, County Report of Leicestershire.*

3. A good introduction to qualitative research can be found in B. Roberts, *Biographical Research* (Buckingham: Open University Press, 2002).
4. See particularly M. K. Dziewanowski, *Poland in the 20th Century* (New York: Columbia University Press, 1977); A. Szczypiorski, *The Polish Ordeal* (London: Croom Helm, 1982); J. Garliński, *Poland in the Second World War* (London: Macmillan, 1985); and N. Davies, *Heart of Europe – A Short History of Poland* (Oxford: Oxford University Press, 1984).
5. M. Winslow, 'Polish Migration to Britain: War, Exile and Mental Health', *Oral History*, 27, 1999, no. 1, pp. 57–64, p. 58. See also M. Hope, *Polish Deportees in the Soviet Union: Origins of Post-war Settlement in Great Britain* (London: Veritas Foundation Publication Centre, 1998); N. S. Lebedeva, 'The Deportation of the Polish Population to the USSR, 1939–41, in A. J. Rieber (ed.), *Communist Studies and Transition Politics*, Special Issue, *Forced Migration in Central and Eastern Europe, 1939–1950*, 16, 2000, nos. 1/2, pp. 28–45.
6. Similar observations about the presentation of war memories can be found in B. Temple, 'Time Travels: Time, Oral History and British-Polish Identities', *Time and Society*, 5, 1996, no. 1, pp. 85–96.
7. Interview with first-generation Polish man, Leicester, 28 February 2001, a.m.
8. Interview with first-generation Polish man, Leicester, 23 August 1999.
9. K. Sword, *Deportation and Exile – Poles in the Soviet Union, 1939–1948* (Basingstoke: Macmillan, 1996), p. 44.
10. First-generation Polish woman, 16 February 2001.
11. Interview with first-generation Polish woman, Leicester, 3 August 1999.
12. First-generation Polish man, 23 August 1999.
13. Interview with first-generation Polish man, Leicester, 28 February 2001, p.m.
14. Interview with first-generation Polish man, Leicester, 26 February 2001.
15. See particularly, N. Davies, *God's Playground, A History of Poland – Volume II, 1795 to the Present* (Oxford: Oxford University Press, 1981).
16. First-generation Polish man, 28 February 2001, p.m.
17. First-generation Polish man, 28 February 2001, p.m.
18. An interesting discussion about the significance of these concepts for Polish national culture can be found in A. Wierzbicka, *Understanding Cultures Through Their Key Words: English, Russian, Polish, German and Japanese* (Oxford: Oxford University Press, 1997), pp. 148–52.
19. Interview with first-generation Polish woman, Leicester, 22 November 2000.
20. Interview with second-generation Polish woman, Leicester, 12 February 2001.
21. Interview with second-generation Polish woman, Leicester, 31 August 1999.
22. Second-generation Polish woman, 12 February 2001.
23. Interview with second-generation Polish woman, Leicester, 9 February 2001.
24. See C. Tighe, *Gdańsk: National Identity in the Polish–German Borderlands* (London: Pluto Press, 1990).
25. Radio Leicester interview with first-generation Polish man, 1995, exact date unknown.
26. Norman Davies provides an interesting consideration of the role of myth in Polish national history in N. Davies, 'Polish National Mythologies', in G. Hosking and G. Schopflin (eds), *Myths and Nationhood* (London: Hurst, 1997), pp. 141–57.
27. Interview with second-generation Polish woman, Leicester, 3 July 2000.
28. Second-generation Polish woman, 9 February 2001.
29. Second-generation Polish woman, 12 February 2001.
30. Interview with first-generation Polish man, Leicester, 26 January 2001.

31. First-generation Polish man, 23 August 1999.
32. B. Anderson, 'Exodus', *Critical Inquiry*, 20, 1994, Winter, pp. 314–27, p. 322.
33. Interview with first-generation Polish woman, Leicester, 2 July 2001.
34. For a detailed analysis of Polish transnational and diasporic connections see K. Burrell, 'Small-scale Transnationalism: Homeland Connections and the Polish 'Community' in Leicester', *International Journal of Population Geography*, (forthcoming, 2003).
35. Second-generation Polish woman, 9 February 2001.
36. Interview with two first-generation Polish women, Leicester, 24 February 2000.
37. Interview with first-generation Polish woman, Leicester, 26 February 2001.
38. Interview with first-generation Polish woman, Leicester, 26 August 1999.
39. First-generation Polish woman, 24 February 2000.
40. First-generation Polish man, 26 January 2001.

8

Oral History and Polish Émigrés in Britain

Michelle Winslow

> It is true that a lot of Poles did suffer when they were younger, the
> effects of war and imprisonment, two years of starvation in Siberia
> or other camps. You shake it off but I think sometimes you push it
> under the carpet and when you get older or you retire, it comes
> out, you reminisce about it.[1]

The extent to which the Second World War has influenced the
lives of Polish émigrés cannot be understated. It is *the* defining
event of their lives. The war tore them away from their homes and
families, made them witnesses and recipients of atrocity, and compelled them to live out their lives away from their homeland. For the
vast majority of Poles in Britain, the traumatic experiences and
painful losses of the past significantly impact on their present, and
have remained prominent in their memories throughout half a
century of settlement.

Whilst Poland was on the 'winning side' at the end of the Second
World War, the Poles who found themselves in Britain in 1945 had
little to celebrate. Collectively, they had experienced the horrors of
the Nazi and Soviet regimes, lost relatives and friends through death
and displacement, lost their homes and their aspirations for the future
and, ultimately, they were 'exiled' in an unfamiliar environment
where they had to begin rebuilding their lives. Britain celebrated on
VE Day, but Poles asked, 'what victory?'[2]

Unsurprisingly, the traumatic histories of Polish émigrés have
adversely affected many of their lives. Since the Second World War,
a high incidence of mental illness has prevailed amongst Poles in
Britain and this chapter discusses doctoral research that has explored

this problem. The project was conducted using oral history methods and presents the past in the words of those who participated in it, and as understood by them.[3] The oral accounts provide further perspectives on the history that compelled the resettlement of Poles away from their homeland, offering insights into the experiences of migration and broadening understandings of related problems and issues. An overview of this research is presented here, drawing on a number of oral accounts to illustrate the impact of the war on Polish émigrés from the 1940s to the present day.

As a research method, oral history offers a unique opportunity to engage in history with the living. Recording life stories with Polish émigrés has produced first-hand accounts of experiences of Nazi and Soviet invasion, of atrocity and forced labour, and of how it felt to fight for Poland's freedom, only to emerge as 'the heaviest loser on the winning side'.[4] Nevertheless, critics of oral history question its validity, asking, 'how do we know that it's true?' Yet the same doubt can be cast upon historical sources in general. Historians who work in paper archives, who sift through reports, letters and diaries, must ask of their sources, 'who wrote it, why was it written, and is it a forgery?' All sources must be handled with care, and oral history is no different in this respect. Oral history does not claim to be absolute truth, but it does provide unique historical insights and is particularly significant in that it has the capacity to convey changes wrought by memory; changes described by Alessandro Portelli as revealing the narrators' effort to 'make sense of the past and to give a form to their lives'.[5]

In the context of research with the Polish émigré population in Britain, oral history has enabled an appreciation of the mental health problems that have been constant among it. Interviewees have included former servicemen and women, displaced persons, concentration camp prisoners, Underground Army members, and survivors of the government-in-exile and their dependants. On the 'caring' side, psychiatrists, social workers, priests and care assistants have taken part. In total, 51 interviews were conducted in England, Scotland and Wales.

Ultimately, the research enabled mental health problems to be located in a historical context, but at the outset of the study it was evident that discussion of psychological matters would be problematic. We live in more enlightened times with regard to understanding mental health, but open discussion is still hampered by stigma. This problem is not exclusive to Polish circles; it extends throughout

British society, but amongst Poles it was certainly not assuaged by a researcher, a relative stranger, who arrived asking questions about mental states. Indeed, in the early days of the study, a fleeting reference to the psychological impact of the past during an interview prompted the swift response: 'Sorry, I am not your problem child!'[6]

Whilst émigrés were initially reluctant to engage in discussion about mental health, they were willing to record their personal histories. It was during these early interviews that a common concern emerged: 'Our memories are dying with us.' An ex-officer explained:

> In ten, fifteen, thirty years, there will be second and third generations of Poles. They'll probably have heard old stories from parents or grandparents, but it's not the same. When you speak to me you get the information from the horse's mouth, so to speak.[7]

With the growing realisation that Polish émigrés wished to preserve their memories, and to do so in English in order to reach a broader audience, the research became increasingly focused on life history. The accounts collected were rich in detail and formed the basis of a book, which met the need to document memories.[8] An unanticipated consequence of working with émigrés on the representation of their history was that trusting relationships between the researcher and the 'researched' were forged. These relationships were later to make discussion of mental health issues possible, enabling deeper insight into the past and highlighting issues that influenced the experience of settlement.

It should be noted that this research does not suggest that the majority of Poles in Britain have experienced mental illness. However, it is generally recognised by psychiatrists that social circumstances and psychological experiences play a major part in engendering mental distress,[9] and due to the enormity of the trauma experienced by Polish émigrés during the war and afterwards, it is likely that in addition to those who have become ill, there are many people whose lives are negatively affected by their memories.

MENTAL HEALTH PROBLEMS IN THE EARLY YEARS

Since the 1940s, mental health problems have been evident amongst Poles in Britain and, at first, were directly associated with experiences of war, trauma, loss and bitterness at the Allied politics that brought about their resettlement in Britain. In later years, and in addition to the distress resulting from the war, connections were also made between mental illness and the reduced social and economic status of most émigrés, and their experiences of discrimination and hostility.

That émigré Poles have suffered a disproportionately high incidence of mental health difficulty throughout their years in Britain is not in dispute. In 1950, an analysis of Ministry of Health records of admissions into psychiatric care revealed that mental illness amongst Poles was an especial problem; Polish admissions were 4.1 per thousand (male 4.42; female 3.78), more than four times higher than the British rate of 0.86 per thousand, and almost twice the rate of 2.6 per thousand for all refugee groups in Britain.[10]

As early as 1943, a neuro-psychiatric division was formed for Polish forces in response to the recognition that amongst Polish troops being moved to Scotland were servicemen in need of psychiatric medical provision. Initially, the division used wards in a British hospital and developed two rehabilitation centres, but after the Allies withdrew recognition from the Polish government-in-exile, in 1945, Polish psychiatric operations were taken over by the British Ministry of Health. In 1947, a special unit, Mabledon, was created in Tunbridge, Kent, for mentally ill Polish servicemen and former serving soldiers.[11]

The Polish exclusivity of the unit was not to last, because the Tunbridge area was without psychiatric services and local patients were admitted into the hospital. The hospital was subsequently requisitioned from the Poles and in 1955 its services were relocated to a hospital near Dartford, retaining the name of Mabledon. The new Mabledon served the whole of Britain's Polish population, whilst also serving the local non-Polish population. Admissions were overwhelmingly of Poles, male and female, although male admissions more than doubled those of women, reflecting the larger male Polish émigré population. Ten per cent were under 21 years old, with the majority being between 40 and 50 years old. Patients were of mixed social class, with previous occupations reported as professors, doctors and manual workers. Amongst the women, 50 per cent had previously been housewives who did not work outside the home.[12]

George Bram was Physician Superintendent of Mabledon, and Inka Nowotna, a social worker, worked with him in the years after the war:

[George Bram] was a marvellous man and marvellous doctor. First of all, he listened to the patients ... he would listen and look at the patient, so the patient always felt important ... He was really interested in his patients and he tried and succeeded in getting the right medication for every patient ... I used to work with Dr Bram at the out-patient clinic in London every Tuesday afternoon. We started at two in the afternoon and we finished, seven, nine, sometimes eleven at night. And the patients who were discharged from Mabledon Hospital and came to London were my responsibility, to look after their welfare, but Mabledon Hospital could admit Polish patients from Sheffield, from Devon, from everywhere.[13]

By 1978, beds were still available for mentally ill Poles at Mabledon, but the number had been greatly reduced, despite Bram's complaints that chronically ill and geriatric cases were increasing:

Each week requests are made to myself and Mrs Nowotna, the Social Worker, for admission to Mabledon, of dementing Poles. Many of them without families ... we must remember that the rate of mental breakdown among refugees is much higher than among the native population ... and the process is accelerating now as the Polish population is ageing.'[14]

During the 1970s, Mabledon was housing patients who had lived there since the 1950s. In 1995, a few of these long-term patients were still being housed in a specialist Polish unit in Dartford, Kent; their entire lives in Britain having been spent receiving hospital care.

MENTAL HEALTH AND THE POLISH ÉMIGRÉ MAJORITY

With the war over, many Poles in Britain were presented with an opportunity to regain a sense of security. Many of the newcomers were young, and found time to rekindle their 'lost youth' by enjoying social time with friends and romantic partners, and by experiencing the excitement of discovering a new country. Yet these were people who had experienced horrific trauma, and many struggled with feelings of guilt for having survived when friends and family had not, and for not returning to surviving family members in Poland. The following interviewee, who was in the Polish Air

Force, explained how he sought professional help for his troubled
state of mind in the late 1940s, with unsatisfactory results:

> I was living another life, I was happy, we had started to plan, yet at
> night I had nightmares, dreams, all towards the war and uncertainty
> about relatives … well anyhow whilst we were living at [a friend's
> house] she realised that I was living through something and she
> advised me to go and see doctor, and for some time I used to go to
> hospital. I think, once a week, for an interview … psychiatrist, to
> help me. But I knew they couldn't help me because I knew what I
> went through. I knew what was the reason for it, but they didn't
> think it was true … Because they weren't aware at that point, they
> didn't know what had gone on in the war … I was haunted by night-
> mares. Nobody knows, only those who went through it.[15]

Illness in the early years can be understood in the context of
traumatic war experience, the crushing blow of exile and struggling
to cope in a new environment, but a more difficult situation to
understand is why the high incidence of mental illness continued.
In 1971, the Polish Ex-Combatants' Association (SPK) voiced its
concerns:

> Mental illness is exceptionally high among refugees. The Polish Ex-
> Combatant's Association, which runs a department for employment
> and assistance, has under its care, in London alone, over a hundred
> mentally disabled. Others are looked after in homes and hostels
> run by the Relief Society for Poles, and within the capability of their
> slender resources, these and other organisations do magnificent
> work.[16]

Philip Rack wrote that the problems of Polish émigrés were related
to their past experiences: trauma; loss; adjusting to a new language
and culture; reduced social and employment status; and facing
hostility in the workplace.[17] Additional hostility in the immediate
post-war years occurred as a result of the housing shortage in Britain.
In some areas, the competition for accommodation led to Poles
being vilified for taking lodgings when the indigenous population
was in need.[18] Such hostility from their wartime allies came as a bitter
blow: 'English person had as a weapon … "go back where you came
from", and it hurt.'[19]

The problems encountered by émigrés as they endeavoured to settle in their new surroundings merged with anguish at the political circumstances that brought about their unwilling resettlement. Reflecting on his early days in Britain, this former Underground Army fighter explained how he and his compatriots felt at the time:

> Our settlement in Britain was made all the more difficult by our feeling of betrayal. The Yalta, Tehran and Potsdam treaties seemed, especially to those who had served in the British services, as a betrayal. The soldiers who had fought in the underground army, and in the Warsaw Uprising of 1944 were now regarded by the Polish-Soviet Communist government as 'enemies of the state'. They were accused of collaboration with the Nazis and other crimes. We read in British and French newspapers of the persecution of AK [Home Army] soldiers still in Poland and we felt extreme bitterness towards our allies who recognised the puppet Polish government which was killing our own people, who had fought for the freedom of our country. Withdrawal of recognition of the legitimate Polish government-in-exile was a bitter blow. We were completely lost and this did not help us to settle. We did not trust our allies any more and no longer felt safe. All this made our settling very problematic.[20]

A further source of bitterness was the exclusion of the Polish Army from the Allied Victory Parade held in London on 8 June 1946. An invitation was extended to 25 Polish airmen who took part in the Battle of Britain, but they refused to attend on the grounds that they could not be present at a ceremony from which the Polish Army was excluded.[21] The situation had more to do with political considerations than any failure to recognise the achievements of the Poles, since the officially recognised Polish government in Warsaw had been invited to send representatives.[22] Nevertheless, the omission was a source of much resentment:

> Most of my compatriots are still very, very bitter about how the Polish forces were treated ... my husband, who was in the Polish army under the British command, was not at the Victory Parade and we felt, well, betrayed, if you want ... Of course, one can understand the political situation was such that Churchill probably didn't have any other choice, but it was very painful and it still is for very elderly people, still is a wound which is not cleaned at all.[23]

Since the 1940s, a steady source of psychological support could be found in the Polish Ex-Servicemen's Clubs. These institutions have been of immense value to the majority of émigrés, and were often an essential 'lifeline' for many former officers. Within the Ex-Servicemen's Club environment self-esteem could be restored, and former officers who were employed as club managers were also able to improve their employment status. Even so, some people experienced severe problems and the plight of many older officers was well known to Inka Nowotna:

> They were called the 'Silver Brigade' ... in hotels, polishing silver, and also silver haired ... in those days a man over sixty was considered to be old, he couldn't be retrained. How can you explain to a full General in the Polish Army that he can do nothing else but polish? ... It was degrading.[24]

GROWING OLDER IN A 'SECOND HOMELAND'

In addition to the difficulties created by war trauma, bitterness and settling in a new environment, further problems developed as Poles aged. Indeed, a particularly vulnerable time for mental health difficulty is after retirement, when contact with colleagues is lost and individuals reach the stage in life where factors such as ill-health, bereavement and children leaving home can produce stress and isolation from the familiar life they previously knew. Isolation amongst ageing Polish émigrés extends beyond the immobilising effects of disability; it can be cultural and linguistic also, adding an extra dimension to the usual problems of ageing. Cultural isolation can be due to severed contact with Polish companions, for whatever reason, whilst linguistic isolation might occur as a result of lost contact with Polish friends and the adoption of a 'British' lifestyle, with the resultant loss of opportunities to talk in Polish.

Unfortunately, there is a tendency for learned languages to diminish with age, and even the most expert English speakers have complained of deteriorating language skills. This problem is more than a nuisance or an embarrassment; the situation heightens feelings of being a foreigner, growing old in a country that is becoming alien all over again. Loss of language makes hard work of everyday life, and further, with a reduced English voice, there is a pressing need to communicate in Polish. Where people have stayed in contact with Polish organisations their language needs can be met; however, there can be unhappy consequences where contact has been lost.

Reminiscence, a familiar process of ageing, can also have embittering consequences. Poles remember being taken from their beds by armed police; horrific deportations into slave labour; empty stomachs; witnessing and experiencing atrocities, lost family and friends and, ultimately, the Allied 'betrayal' that brought about their exile. Happier memories can be overshadowed by a need to make sense of past events. Reminiscence can also bring self-recrimination, however misplaced this might appear in reality. The following extract was contributed by an interviewee who was just ten years old when the war started, and whose education suffered as a result. He assisted the Underground Army during the Warsaw Rising, was imprisoned in Germany, and later came to Britain with the Polish Forces. He resumed his education in England, but struggled to attend night school in a second language, and after a shift in a coal mine. Additionally, as an 18-year-old who had recently been released from Dachau, his need for education was in conflict with his need for enjoyment. Throughout his life, his belief that he had under-achieved remained a source of regret:

> I could have probably made something better of myself. I've wasted the little talent I've had just for simple manual jobs … My mother [in Poland] never knew, I could never tell her that I went down coal mine. When she did ask me what I'm doing, I told her … I told her that I'm working in an engineering firm. Never told her the truth, it would have broke her heart.[25]

To combat the negative effects of distressing memories such as these, there is therapeutic value to be gained from talking in Polish with someone who has lived through the same events. In a residential home for Poles in Yorkshire, a Polish-speaking social worker was well aware of the need to reminisce amongst residents:

> We would sit at dinner and somebody would say something about Siberia … 'when I was in Siberia'. And then another lady would say something and suddenly there was this discussion with them all talking about their lives. Then one would cry and another would

start crying and I'd say, 'ok, we won't talk about this, these sad things, we'll talk about something else now.' And they would say, 'no, no, we have to talk about it, I want to talk about it.' And no matter how much they cried they wanted to talk about how their mother and father had died in Siberia, and children and, you know, everything. They had to talk about it.[26]

However, not all Polish émigrés have access to an empathetic Polish ear. There are also people who have never spoken about their painful experiences and probably never will. In other situations, non-Polish partners might be unsupportive should their spouses want to renew their acquaintance with their Polish cultural background. Immobility further prevents older Poles from meeting together, and few local authorities provide transport to Polish centres. Whilst professional opinion supports talking, this apparently uncomplicated therapy is thus not always an option.

This study supports the view that talking about traumatic personal histories promotes a process of coming to terms with the past, but it also recognises that this process might never be completed, as the past has left indelible scars in the memories of Polish émigrés:

> We are resilient up to a point, we can stand a lot and still survive, but somehow you have to pay for it. It comes back, you have night-mares, sometimes you experience fear, for no reason at all. It is a fear that somehow you experienced in the past and it is still there, still persisting.[27]

Certainly, there are many Polish émigrés who have managed their lives well, and are still able to do so. However, the likelihood of psychological problems occurring in this group of people is higher than amongst the wider population. Problems, when they arise, are a complex mix of needing to come to terms with a traumatic past and of coping with the present. And language loss is a huge problem that marks out older Poles as foreigners in a country that they fought for and that has been their adopted homeland for over fifty years.

The issues raised here link memory and identity in particular. Those who are able to talk about the past in Polish, as happens in Polish social clubs throughout Britain, have an understanding of who they are and will talk about the miscarriages of justice that have shaped their lives. Indeed, for the vast majority, the war is the most significant event they have ever experienced. It is the reason why they live in Britain and the reason why their lives have taken the shape they have. Subsequent experiences have been fashioned from that catastrophic event: work, marriage, children, friends, retirement and, in due course, coming to terms with dying a thousand miles away from your homeland.

Having opportunities to tell and retell life stories, or parts of life stories, enables a process of making sense of this past, and talking with others is an important safety valve. However, where this process is prevented by isolation, loss of language or some other reason, coming to terms with the past can be very difficult. The motivation of many émigrés who agreed to be involved with this oral history study can be linked with the process of needing to come to terms with the past. Painful memories can be seen to have a 'useful' purpose when left as evidence, or as a warning from history, or as commemoration of the dead. Gaining an opportunity to record memories for historical record enables validation of personal experiences.

The previously discussed émigré, who told of not revealing his employment status to his mother in Poland, provided a poignant example of the need to bear witness to a traumatic past. Following his interview in 1996, which included painful memories of the Warsaw Rising and imprisonment in a death camp, he kept in touch with the study but eventually lost contact in 1999. In November 2000, he was prompted to make contact again on becoming aware that an exhibition based on oral history collected during the course of research was in preparation.[28] By this time, he was seriously ill in hospital but wanted to discuss the interview that he had given years earlier, and requested that his story be represented in the exhibition, as it was. Shortly after this meeting he died, but with the knowledge that his experiences would not die with him.

Recall of the past is a normal part of human mental activity; it is something that people do throughout their lives. However, in old age, reminiscence has a more developed role and perhaps more significant outcomes.[29] Amongst Polish émigrés, ongoing analysis of life events helps individuals to make sense of the past, and from a mental health perspective, talking in this way provides an important safety valve. However, where this process is prevented by isolation and loss of language, it can be assumed that coming to terms with the past might be difficult and tortuous.

Much of this discussion refers to the situations of 'ordinary' age-ing Poles, yet the likelihood of psychological problems occurring amongst this group is higher than in most other migrant groups and markedly higher than the indigenous British-born population. When problems occur, they are a combination of needing to come to terms with a traumatic past and coping with present difficulties. The war created psychological casualties, but fifty years on, problems are still evident and the past is very much a part of the present for many Poles living in Britain today.

NOTES

1. Recorded by M. Winslow, 5 December 1997, Tape 17.
2. Personal communication with Polish ex-servicemen, 8 May 1995. This date marked the 50th anniversary of the end of the Second World War in Europe.
3. M. Winslow, 'War, resettlement, rooting and ageing: An oral history study of Polish émigrés in Britain', Ph.D. thesis, Department of History, University of Sheffield, May 2001.
4. A. Suchcitz, *Poland's Contribution to the Allied Victory in the Second World War* (London: Polish Ex-Combatants' Association in Great Britain, 1995), p. 16.
5. A. Portelli, 'What makes oral history different', R. Perks and A. Thomson (eds), *The Oral History Reader* (London: Routledge, 1998), pp. 68–9.
6. Personal communication with M. Winslow, 4 April 1996.
7. Recorded by M. Winslow, 8 June 1998, Tape 29.
8. A book based on the oral history collected during this research was produced towards the end of the study: T. Smith, M. Winslow, *Keeping the Faith: The Polish Community in Britain,* (Bradford: Bradford Heritage Recording Unit, 2000).
9. T. Heller, J. Reynolds, R. Gomm, R. Muston, S. Pattison (eds), 'The nature of psychiatric disorders', *Mental Health Matters: A Reader* (Basingstoke: Macmillan, in association with the Open University, 1996), pp. 17–26.
10. J. Zubrzycki, *Polish Immigrants in Britain. A Study of Adjustment* (The Hague: Martinus Nijhoff, 1956), pp. 186–7.
11. Unpublished report, 'Mabledon', p. 24. The report is undated and without a name. It is likely that it was produced in the early 1970s, with G. Bram as the author. Copy in possession of M. Winslow.
12. Ibid., pp. 7, 22–5.
13. Recorded by M. Winslow, 13 March 1999, Tape 44.
14. Unpublished source: 'Memo: Re Mabledon Hospital', by G. Bram, Hon. Consultant Psychiatrist to the Dartford and Gravesham Group of Hospitals. 13 June 1978. Copy in possession of M. Winslow.
15. Recorded by M. Winslow, 31 January 1998, Tape 18.
16. Polish Ex-Combatants' Association, *The Poles in Great Britain 1971* (London: Polish Ex-Combatants' Association, 1971), p. 6.
17. P. Rack, *Race, Culture and Mental Disorder* (London: Routledge, 1993) p. 27.
18. C. Holmes, *A Tolerant Country? Immigrants, Refugees and Minorities in Britain,* (London: Faber, 1991), p. 47.
19. Recorded by M. Winslow, 2 October 1997, Tape 11.

20. Personal correspondence with M. Winslow, 6 January 1999.
21. W. Anders, *An Army in Exile: The Story of the Second Polish Corps* (London: Macmillan, 1949), p. 299.
22. J. Hanson, 'Sympathy, Antipathy, Hostility: British attitudes to non-repatriable Poles and Ukrainians after the Second World War and to the Hungarian refugees of 1956', Ph.D. thesis, Department of History, University of Sheffield, June 1995, p. 196.
23. Recorded by M. Winslow, 13 March 1999, Tape 44.
24. Ibid.
25. Recorded by M. Winslow, 14 August 1996, Tape 4.
26. Recorded by M. Winslow, 29 December 1999, Tape 47.
27. Recorded by M. Winslow, 5 December 1997, Tape 17.
28. The exhibition, 'Keeping the Faith: The Polish Community in Britain', was produced by T. Smith and M. Winslow and accompanied the publication of the same name: see note 8.
29. J. Bornat, 'Oral History as a Social Movement', Perks and Thomson, *Oral History Reader*, p. 201.

9

The Polish Institute and Sikorski Museum and its Archival Holdings

Andrzej Suchcitz

With the closing months of the Second World War, it was clear that its eventual end would not restore Poland's independence. The Yalta Conference of February 1945 simply confirmed and made public the decisions reached at Tehran in late 1943. Poland's Western allies had agreed to the Soviet Union annexing the eastern half of Poland, compensating the latter westwards and leaving the country firmly within the Soviet sphere of influence. For the Polish state authorities in exile and the majority of armed forces personnel and their dependents, in total over 250,000 people in 1945, the fight to regain Poland's freedom continued, albeit in a different form. Among the myriad matters to be resolved was the question of the future of the state archives, both of the civilian ministries as well as the armed forces, not to mention the vast collection of historical exhibits collected during the war with the idea of replenishing, in part, the looted musuems and collections in Poland.

The initiative to create a historical institute to house both archives and exhibits came from Lt.-Col. Zygmunt Borkowski, head of the Armed Forces Archive and Museum Service. On the advice of British friends, the planned institute had all the hallmarks of a private organisation. On no account could it be a state institute, as this would open the way to the likely possibility of the new, communist regime in Warsaw trying to lay claim to it, something with which the British government would feel obliged to concur.[1]

On 2 May 1945, the deeds of trust of the General Sikorski Historical Institute were signed. On the basis of this, Helena Sikorska, the widow of the Polish Prime Minister and Commander-in-Chief, donated to the Institute her husband's memorabilia. The organising committee, formed of 12 persons, both Polish and British and one American, became the Institute's first council. At its head stood the chairman of the Scottish-Polish Society, the Earl of Elgin and Kincardine, an old and trusted friend of Poland. The day-to-day running of the new institution lay in the hands of the executive committee. Its first chairman was Stanisław Stroński, Professor of French Literature and politician who had served as Deputy Prime Minister and Minister of Information and Documentation in Sikorski's wartime cabinets. Lt.-Col. Borkowski became the Institute's director. After Professor Stroński's resignation in 1951, he was succeeded as chairman by General Professor Marian Kukiel, followed by General Sikorski's son-in-law, Stanisław Leśniowski, and lastly by Captain Ryszard Dembiński.

In 1946, the present building of the Institute, at 20 Prince's Gate, was purchased for £13,000 from Lord Woodbridge, a former mayor of Ipswich, MP and Vice-chairman of the British–American Tobacco Company Ltd. The initial financing of the Institute came from the funds of the Polish Second Corps (£10,000) and the remainder of the Polish Armed Forces (£10,000), as well as the Interim Treasury Committee for Polish Affairs, which provided £5,000. Until 1949, some of the staff were financed through their postings with the Polish Resettlement Corps. This came to a halt in 1949. Henceforth, the Institute had to rely solely on its own ability to attract donations. It is very important to underline that throughout its 57 years the Institute has been self-financing, relying on membership subscriptions, donations and bequests. At no time did it receive any official state funding, thereby retaining full control of its affairs. Not only does the Institute rely to this day on voluntary subscriptions, but this extends to the work carried out in all the departments – the Archives, Museum, Library and Administration. At present, there are only two persons employed by the Institute, while the remaining eighty-plus staff are all volunteers who give their time freely. For example, in the Archives there are 25 volunteers who come regularly, some for a couple of hours a week, others for a couple of days per week.[2]

In 1965, the General Sikorski Historical Institute and the Polish Research Centre, which had been established in London at the end of 1939, were amalgamated to form the Polish Institute and Sikorski Museum, the name by which it is known to this day. In 1970, the

Regimental Colours Fund was set up. Its main task, apart from financing the repairs and care of individual army colours, was to create a large enough fund to cover all the costs of maintaining the Institute's building.

In 1973, the Polish Historical Institute, which had played a dual role, that of the General Staff Historical Commission as well as a cover for a nucleus General Staff in exile in the late 1940s and 1950s, became part of the Institute. Its main task remained, and remains, to complete the monumental official history of the Polish Armed Forces during the Second World War.[3] In 1988, the Polish Underground Movement (1939–1945) Study Trust, which existed since 1947 as a separate independent archive, became an autonomous body within the Institute. Its documentation neatly complements that of the Institute, as is shown below.

Although the Institute came into existence in 1945, it was many years before the bulk of the documentation was actually deposited at 20 Prince's Gate and made fully available to reseachers. The necessity of the latter was quickly seen by the first Keeper of Archives, Dr Edmund Oppman. During his brief tenure as Keeper (he died in 1951), the initial foundations were laid on which his sucessors built. He saw the need to begin the task of sorting out the documents held, because an 'Archive is not a storage place but an institution which from its various bricks, i.e. documents, builds a lasting edifice upon which is based the history of a bygone era.'

The documentation of the Polish Armed Forces was the first to be taken over by the Institute, in 1947. The question of the governmental archives was more complex because, while much reduced in scope, the Polish government-in-exile continued to exist and function.[4] Despite clear directives by the President of the Republic and a cabinet decision that all state papers pertaining to the war be taken over by the Institute, it was many years before it could be said that the majority of individual ministry archives had been given to it. With all the confusion following the end of the war, and the uncertainty as to the individual future of government officials who now had to build new lives for themselves and their families, it is not altogether surprising that archival problems were relegated to the bottom of the pile. This had the unfortunate consequence that many of the archives of individual ministries were handed over in a very incomplete form. For example, parts of the Foreign Ministry archive for 1945 surfaced in the late 1970s, when

the building in which they had been deposited, belonging to the
Archbishop of Westminster, was being renovated.

It must also be remembered that parts of the wartime government
papers were taken over by the communist regime in Warsaw, as a
result of individual civil servants and politicians going over to their
service and taking with them any documents of interest to the
communist authorities that they could collect – most often, in the
form of fragmentary archives. During the late 1950s and 1960s, the
Polish government-in-exile deposited large amounts of ministerial
archives with the Hoover Institution in California, unfortunately not
securing ownership titles to them for the long run.[5]

The last major takeover of government archives came in 1991–92,
following the liquidation of the Polish state-in-exile and the winding-
up of the Presidential Office, the Prime Minister's Office, and of
the individual ministries and state institutions. Theoretically, the
documentation that arrived then covered the post-war period of the
government-in-exile's activity. In reality, there were a number of files
going back to the wartime period.

Overall, this means that the wartime archives of the Polish
government and, to a much lesser degree, of the Armed Forces are
held by three institutions: the Polish Institute and Sikorski Museum
in London, the Archives of Contemporary Records in Warsaw and
the Hoover Institution in Stanford, California. However, it is the
Archives of the Institute in London that form the bulk of the
collection, and any student/researcher interested in the role of
the Polish government during the Second World War and that of the
Polish Armed Forces should make use of this rich source. It would
be impossible to write something purporting to be based on available
material without including it.

Taken in their entirety, the holdings of the Archives of the Polish
Insititute and Sikorski Museum extend to over 1.5. kilometers of
shelving. The documents held basically cover three distinct periods
in Polish history. The first is that of the First World War and
independence up until the fall of Poland in early October 1939.
Putting aside the actual Polish campaign, these materials are highly
fragmentary, the majority having been evacuated in September 1939
by the military authorities. Despite their noticeable fragmentation
and incompleteness, they nevertheless constitute an important
primary source for those interested in the period. As far as the
civilian documentation is concerned, the most extensive for this

period comes from individual diplomatic missions. Of special value are the papers of the Polish Legation (from 1929, the Polish Embassy) in London, which include a complete set of telegrams between the Foreign Ministry in Warsaw and the mission, covering the period 1919–39.[6] Interestingly enough, scattered documentation from the period of the First World War can be found among the papers of the Polish Consulate-General in London. These pertain to help given to Polish refugees and prisoners of war held in Britain as captured soldiers of the German and Austrian armies. Especially active here was the daughter of the artist, Sir Laurence Alma-Tadema.[7] The papers of the Embassy to the Holy See for the 1930s provide interesting insights into Polish–Vatican relations, as well as Poland's relations with her minorites, notably the Ukrainians.[8] There is a smattering of pre-war papers in the Madrid Legation grouping. Together with the papers of the Military Attaché's office in Lisbon for this period, they provide unknown material concerning the Spanish Civil War (1936–39).[9]

Particularly noteworthy towards the end of the period are the papers of the individual directorates of the Polish General Staff, most notably of the Directorate of Military Operations and the Directorate of Military Intelligence. The latter include the annual reports of the Military Attaché in Berlin, as well as his reports on specific aspects of Germany's military machine. Of primary importance are the papers concerning the run-up to war and of the 1939 campaign itself. In many cases these are quite unique. The Institute's holdings of documents of the Polish High Command from the campaign itself are the largest held anywhere. They are divided into daily subgroups, each beginning with the Commander-in-Chief, descending to the various offices of the General Staff and Ministry of War, through files for individual armies in the field and ending with various military districts in the rear lines of communication. These include units that met the invading Red Army and provided initial confirmation of the Soviet invasion on 17 September 1939. This grouping includes daily conversations by teleprinter beteween Marshal Śmigły-Rydz, the Polish Commander-in-Chief, and his army commanders in the field. This provides authentic information and atmosphere as known at a given time during the campaign.[10] The 1939 documents are complemented by several thousand depositions written for the Commission Investigating the Causes of the 1939 defeat. Although often biased and tendentious, they provide a wealth of information not only on the campaign itself, but the military preparations made before the outbreak of war.[11] All the above army materials have their equivalents in the air force and navy groups of documents.

There is little doubt that the largest part of the Archive is devoted to the period of the Polish government's and Armed Forces' activities in exile, first in France, and from June 1940 in Britain. It is impossible to cover all the groupings held, and only the most important will be mentioned here. The starting point for any reseacher must be the war diary of General Władysław Sikorski (1881–1943). This massive work was prepared in the mid-1940s by Regina Oppman, who was Keeper of Archives from 1951 to 1980. It gives a daily itinerary of whom Sikorski saw as Prime Minister and Commander-in-Chief from 1939 to 1943. Supplemented by selected documents, press cuttings and photographs, the war diary in 47 monthly volumes provides the basis for any biography of the General as a wartime leader.

The single most important, central group of papers are those of the Cabinet Office, providing a rich source of material for the political, diplomatic and military policy pursued by the Polish state-in-exile. This is the starting point for any attempt to write a wartime history of Poland. All the various threads of policies pursued, relations with the underground authorities in occupied Poland, relations with the Allied great powers, internal Polish relations, relations *vis-à-vis* the minorities, meet in the Cabinet Office.[12] It is worth noting that the minutes of the meetings of the Council of Ministers for the wartime period are currently being published in their entirety. To date, five volumes have come out,[13] and a further three are planned.

A similar, if not quite as important, archival group is the Chancellery of the President of the Republic. As in the Cabinet Office archive, the reseacher can find here the multiple facets of the government's and army's policies and activities.

Alongside these groupings mention must be made of the mini-parliament-in-exile, the National Council, whose stenograms of plenary sessions as well as those of its various commissions make fascinating reading.[14] For students of Poland's foreign relations, the files of the Ministry of Foreign Affairs, together with those of the individual diplomatic missions, are of central importance. It must be said that, to a certain extent, the Polish Embassy in London took over the role of the ministry, at times overshadowing it. Thus many aspects of Poland's foreign policy other than Anglo–Polish relations can be found in the embassy files. A small part of the Polish embassy in Kuybyshev provides interesting material for Polish–Soviet relations, as well as the network of embassy delegations in the Soviet Union's eastern countries that from 1941 provided welfare for Poles who had been deported by the Soviet Secret Police (NKVD) between 1939 and 1941. Especially poignant are the addresses and appeals by the civilian population and children to the government and President. On the basis of the above archives, the Institute published a two-volume selection of documents on Polish–Soviet relations 1939–45.[15]

For the student of military history, the collections of the Institute are particularly rich and fascinating. Moreover, these are papers that, in contrast to the political ones, are requested far less infrequently. Although much was destroyed during the evacuation from France in June 1940, there is a core of papers on the history of the Polish Army in France, its organisation, build-up and eventually its combat record. The latter is best covered by the papers of the Independent Podhalańska Rifle Brigade, which fought at Narvik, and of the 1st Grenadiers Division during the French campaign in 1940. For the latter, most of the existing material is in the form of written depositions.[16]

With the evacuation of the remnants of the Polish forces from France to the United Kingdom, the process of rebuilding them began anew. There are large groupings covering the First Corps in Scotland, the Independent Carpathian Rifles Brigade, including the defence of Tobruk, the Polish Army in the Soviet Union that was formed in 1941 from prisoners and deportees taken during the 1939 campaign and subsequent occupation of eastern Poland; this army's evacuation to Persia and the formation of the Polish Army in the Middle East, as well as its operational arm, the Second Corps, whose documentation covers all aspects of the Italian campaign involving Polish troops. Meanwhile, back in Scotland, the First Airborne Brigade and First Armoured Division were formed, trained and sent into battle, the former at Arnhem, the latter in the north-west Europe campaign.

Historians of all these battles will find a wealth of contemporary source material that has not often been tapped by English-language writers. Not only do these materials provide a different angle on these well-known battles, but in more than one case unique material not available in British archives. It goes without saying that the majority of documentation is in Polish, but for the patient researcher much material in English is also available. Of inestimable value, both as a source of information about particular units and often as an illustrative source, are the hundreds of unit chronicles and war diaries. These, in particular, are a veritable gold mine for a multitude of reasons, not least for local historians. This is especially true of the chronicles of units of the First Corps stationed in Scotland. It would be difficult to find a corner of Scotland where Polish forces had not been stationed at one time or another. Descriptions of local garrisons, local press clippings, often photographs – important for the local histories of these towns and villages – abound on the pages of these chronicles.

Of central importance among the papers of the Polish Armed Forces are those of the High Command, that is, of the General Staff and Ministry of Defence. Together, they form 91 subgroups, each containing from one to over two hundred files. Here are covered all the central military institutions, including the Directorates of Operations, Organisation and, above all, Intelligence, which provided the Allies with a constant flow of valuable information about troop movements, build-ups, armament production and secret weapons, including the V1 and V2 rockets. The Military Technical Institute sheds interesting light on Polish wartime inventions, including the no. 3 Polish mine detector, which was used throughout the British Army.

There are separate collections about the Polish Navy and Polish Air Force. Each is divided into subsections covering their respective commands, training schools and, above all, individual operational units. In the case of the navy, each warship is covered by anything up to fifty files, whilst each squadron of the Polish Air Force has an extensive collection of files on organisational, training, personnel and operational aspects. Again, the most interesting materials can be found in the squadron chronicles and war diaries.

An aspect of the documentation held, little known and almost totally ignored by British historians, is the wealth of biographical material for various high-ranking British, American and Allied politicians and commanders. Their correspondence can be found in countless files in the Institute archives.[17]

Although the fighting ended in 1945, the Second World War military collections carry on until the disbandment of the Polish Armed Forces within the framework of the Polish Resettlement Corps. All the political, military and social problems resulting from Poland's political defeat in the last war are evident in these immediate post-war papers.

As mentioned, the Polish state structures did not evaporate into thin air at the end of the war. The papers of the government-in-exile, covering the Presidential Chancellery, Prime Minister's Office, individual ministries and the National Council, as well as the papers of the National Unity Executive and Council of Three during the period of duality in the state structures that existed between 1954 and 1972, make for fascinating reading about a community in political exile, its motivations and actions aimed at regaining independence for Poland. Both for the war period as well as afterward, there is a wealth of information regarding Polish schools – one of the largest unsung single achievements during the tempestuous years of war and exile. Wherever a Polish community was established, one of the first things to be organised were classes and schools for children. Despite the Poles' reputation for military prowess and bravery, their concern for the education of the young was second to none.[18]

The single largest part of the Archive enjoying continual growth is the collections, both of individuals and of organisations that have long since been wound up or are coming to the end of their existence. There are presently 611 such collections. They cover the whole gamut of topics mentioned, as well as others. The researcher will find here documents dating from the nineteenth century up to the present day. All fields are covered: politics, the military, diplomacy, economics, academia, literature, the arts, journalism. There are collections of heads of state (for example, Presidents August Zaleski and Edward Raczyński), politicans, generals, senior and junior officers, writers, economists, diplomats, artists, university professors, non-commissioned officers and many others. Numerous memoirs, official and private correspondence make up an essential source for any serious historian. All professions are represented, as are all social classes.[19]

When speaking of the Institute's archival holdings, mention must be made of Captain Wacław Milewski, who, first as the Deputy Keeper of Archives and then as Keeper of Archives from 1980–89, was the driving force in creating the Archives in their present form. His contribution to their organisation, cataloguing and availability for reseachers, be they professional historians or amateur family geneologists, cannot be overestimated.

As already noted, in 1988 the Archives of the Polish Underground Movement Study Trust augmented the collections of the Institute, whilst retaining its autonomy. The Study Trust Archives are based primarily on the documentation of the VIth Special Directorate of the Polish General Staff, which was responsible for all communications between GHQ in London and GHQ Home Army in Warsaw, as well as of the Social Department of the Ministry of the Interior, which had responsibility for communications between the government in London and the government delegation in occupied Poland. This archive holds general and detailed reports about the political, military, economic and social situation in the occupied country. For the period of Operation Tempest, in 1944–45, there are thousands of cyphers from the regional district Home Army commands documenting the process of the introduction of the so-called liberation – the instalment of the new forces of occupation – those of the Soviet Union, with the aid of their Polish collaborators. The process of the annexation and destruction of the vestiges of Polish life in eastern Poland is dramatically conveyed in these despatches. It is possible to follow in similar detail, nearly on an hourly basis, the Warsaw Rising of 1944. It makes for poignant reading.[20]

The Archive's collections are an immense treasure trove of Polish and European, even of world history, which for over half a century carried the torch for freedom of access to Polish archives, at a time when Poland was in the grip of Soviet-controlled censorship, not only of history but of access to historical sources.

NOTES

1. A. Suchcitz, 'Powstanie Instytutu Historycznego im. Gen. Sikorskiego w Londynie 1945–1949', in *Idea Europy i Polska w XIX–XX wieku* (Wrocław: 1999), p. 184.
2. *Sprawozdanie z działalności Instytutu Polskiego i Muzeum im. gen. Sikorskiego, od 1.1.2000–31.12.2000* (London: Polish Institute and Sikorski Museum, 2001), p.12 (English summary pp. 50–51).
3. *Polskie Siły Zbrojne w drugiej wojnie światowej*, vol. I: *Kampania Wrześniowa 1939 roku, części 1–6,* (London: 1951–2001); vol. II: *Kampania na Obczyźnie, części 1–2,* (London: 1959–75) (3 pending); vol. III: *Armia Krajowa* (London: 1950).
4. *Materiały do dziejów polskiego uchodźctwa niepodległościowego 1945–1990*, editor-in-chief, Józef Jasnowski, vols I–VIII (London: Polish Institute and Sikorski Museum, 1994–99).
5. W. Stępniak, *Archiwalia polskie w zbiorach Instytutu Hoovera Uniwersytetu Stanford* (Warsaw: 1997), pp. 10–14; Archive of the Polish Institute and Sikorski Museum (APISM), PRM.Kol.103. Minutes of the Cabinet meetings of the Polish government-in-exile, 11 November 1958 and 5 August 1959.
6. APISM, archival ref.no: A.12P and A.12.53/1–26.
7. APISM, archival ref.no: A.42/files 247–87, 318–35.
8. APISM, archival ref. no. A.44/122/files 1–20.
9. APISM, archival ref. no. A.45/subgroups 1, 7, 10 and 82 and A.I.2/1–6.

10. APISM, archival ref. no. A.II subgroups 9 onwards.
11. APISM, archival ref. no: B.I subgroups 1 to 127.
12. APISM, archival grouping ref. no: PRM; PRM.K; PRM.E.
13. W. Rojek, A. Suchcitz (eds), *Protokoły z posiedzeń Rady Ministrów Rzeczypospolitej Polskiej 1939–1945* (Kraków: 1994–2001). Vol. 6 covering the period July 1943–April 1944 is due out in 2003.
14. APISM, archival ref. no. A.5. subgroups 1–13.
15. *Documents on Polish–Soviet Relations 1939–1945* (London: General Sikorski Historical Institute; Polish Institute and Sikorski Museum); vol. I (1961), vol. II (1967).
16. APISM, archival ref. for whole group is A.IV.
17. For example, the correspondence of Winston Churchill, Anthony Eden, Lord Selborne, General Sir Alan Brooke, General Sir Bernard Montgomery, General Sir Bernard Paget, Air Chief Marshal Sir Charles Portal, Admiral Sir Max Horton – all British wartime leaders whose correspondence can be found in the Institute's archives.
18. APISM, archival ref. no.: A.19 (Ministry of Religious Affairs and Education), A.74 (Delegation of the Ministry of Religious Affairs and Education in the Middle East).
19. W. Milewski, A. Suchcitz, A. Gorczycki, *Guide to the Archives of the Polish Institute and Sikorski Museum*, vol. I (London: Orbis Books, 1985), covers 49 government archival groups and 273 collections. Currently, these figures have risen to 80 and 611, respectively, without taking the archive groupings of the armed forces into account.
20. A. Suchcitz, *Informator Studium Polski Podziemnej* (London: Studium Polski Podziemnej, 1997). An extensive English summary of the institution's history and a guide to its archival holdings can be found on pages 159–200.

Index